CW00486691

CALABRI

TRAVEL GUIDE

2023 & Beyond

Discover the Allure of Southern Italy's Calabria Region

Ted Paul

All rights reserved. No part of this book may be reproduced, stored in a retrieval system, or transmitted in any form or by any means, electronic, mechanical, photocopying, recording, or otherwise, without the prior written permission of the copyright owner. The information contained in this book is for general information purposes only. The author and publisher make no representations or warranties of any kind, express or implied, about the completeness, accuracy, reliability, suitability or availability with respect to the book or the information, products, services, or related graphics contained in the book for any purpose. Any reliance you place on such information is therefore strictly at your own risk.

Copyright © 2023 by Ted Paul.

TABLE OF CONTENT

Introduction

Welcome to Calabria

We invite you to embark on a captivating journey to the enchanting region of Calabria, nestled in the southern part of Italy. As you turn the pages of this travel guide, prepare to unlock the door to a world of hidden treasures and untold stories. Calabria, often referred to as Italy's hidden gem, is a destination that radiates with a magical charm and captivates the hearts of those who venture here.

Imagine azure coastlines that stretch as far as the eye can see, adorned with pristine sandy beaches and secluded coves lapped by crystal-clear waters. Picture yourself strolling through ancient streets lined with centuries-old buildings, where the echoes of history whisper in your ears. Envision lush green landscapes, where mountains rise majestically, adorned with dense forests, picturesque lakes, and cascading waterfalls.

Calabria's natural beauty is a sight to behold, with its dramatic landscapes encompassing both mountains and sea. The region boasts three national parks, including the magnificent Sila National Park, a vast wilderness dotted with serene lakes, dense forests, and charming mountain villages. Aspromonte National Park, with its rugged terrain and panoramic vistas, offers an unparalleled sense of adventure and exploration.

But Calabria's allure goes beyond its breathtaking scenery. It is a land steeped in rich history, where ancient civilizations have left their indelible mark. From the well-preserved Greek temples of Locri to the impressive Norman castles that dot the landscape, history aficionados will find themselves immersed in a tapestry of tales from bygone eras. Walk in the footsteps of ancient Greeks, Romans, and Byzantines, and let the remnants of their civilizations transport you to a time long past.

Yet, it is not only the landscapes and historical sites that make Calabria special. It is the warmth and hospitality of its people that truly sets it apart. Calabrians are known for their genuine friendliness and welcoming nature, always ready to share their traditions, stories, and delicious cuisine. Indulge in the flavors of Calabrian gastronomy, renowned for its simplicity and authenticity. From fiery 'nduja, a spicy cured pork spread, to fresh seafood delicacies, such as swordfish and anchovies, every bite tells a tale of tradition and passion.

As you traverse the towns and villages of Calabria, you will encounter local festivals that celebrate age-old customs, vibrant music, and exuberant dance. Join in the festivities, and let the rhythmic beats of the tarantella ignite your spirit. Witness the colorful processions that honor patron saints and partake in age-old rituals that have survived the test of time.

Calabria is a place where natural beauty, rich history, and warm hospitality come together in perfect harmony. It is a realm of discovery, where each step reveals a new wonder, and every interaction leaves a lasting impression. So, prepare to be enchanted as you explore Calabria's hidden gems, delve into its ancient past, savor its culinary delights, and connect with the soul of this remarkable region. The secrets of Calabria await, ready to be unveiled by intrepid travelers like yourself. Let the journey begin.

Why Visit Calabria?

Calabria, though less renowned than popular Italian destinations like Tuscany or Sicily, possesses an undeniable allure that stems from its lesser-known status. This hidden gem is precisely what makes it a captivating and enticing destination for travelers seeking an authentic Italian experience away from the crowds of mainstream tourism.

Calabria's uniqueness lies in its ability to offer an unspoiled and genuine glimpse into the heart of Italy. As you venture through the region, you'll encounter a wealth of captivating sights and experiences that remain off the beaten path. From picturesque coastal marvels to awe-inspiring landscapes and centuries-old towns, Calabria unfolds like a well-kept secret waiting to be discovered.

The coastal areas of Calabria boast a plethora of mesmerizing beaches that rival any found in more popular tourist destinations. The Tyrrhenian and Ionian coastlines are adorned with pristine stretches of sand and crystal-clear turquoise waters, inviting visitors to bask in the sun's warmth or indulge in invigorating water activities. These coastal regions are dotted with charming seaside towns and fishing villages, where you can immerse yourself in the laid-back atmosphere and savor the local way of life.

Calabria's landscapes are a testament to nature's artistic prowess. From rugged mountains to rolling hills, verdant valleys to cascading waterfalls, the region's natural beauty leaves a lasting impression. The Sila National Park, with its dense forests, serene lakes, and abundant wildlife, offers a haven for nature lovers and outdoor enthusiasts. In contrast, the Aspromonte National Park captivates with its untamed wilderness, rugged peaks, and panoramic vistas that will leave you breathless.

The ancient towns of Calabria are steeped in history, with remnants of civilizations that have shaped the region over the centuries. Wander through the narrow cobblestone streets of Reggio Calabria, where the Museo Nazionale della Magna Grecia showcases artifacts from the ancient Greek colonies. Explore the charming medieval village of Tropea, perched high above the sea and adorned with architectural gems such as Tropea Cathedral and Santa Maria dell'Isola. Cosenza, with its medieval architecture and historic landmarks like the Cosenza Cathedral and Rendano Theatre, offers a glimpse into the region's rich cultural heritage.

Calabria's vibrant local culture is best experienced through its traditional festivals, where the spirit of the community comes alive with music, dance, and gastronomic delights. These festivities offer a window into the authentic traditions and customs that have been preserved for generations. The region's cuisine is a true reflection of its cultural heritage, with a focus on fresh local ingredients and bold flavors. Indulge in the tantalizing tastes of Calabrian cuisine, characterized by fiery chili peppers, exquisite cured meats, artisanal cheeses, and delectable seafood dishes.

Beyond its captivating coastal marvels, breathtaking landscapes, ancient towns, and vibrant local culture, Calabria holds a special charm that sets it apart from its more renowned Italian counterparts.

One of the standout features of Calabria is its sense of tranquility. Unlike the bustling tourist hotspots, Calabria offers a peaceful and serene atmosphere, allowing you to truly unwind and connect with the beauty of your surroundings. Whether you find solace on a secluded beach, hike through a quiet forest, or explore a historic village without the crowds, Calabria provides a respite from the fast-paced world and invites you to slow down and appreciate the simple pleasures of life.

Another remarkable aspect of Calabria is its authenticity. This region has managed to retain its traditional way of life, largely untouched by modernization. As you explore the towns and interact with the locals, you'll discover a genuine warmth and sincerity that embodies the true spirit of Italy. From the friendly conversations with artisans in the bustling markets to the heartfelt hospitality of family-run agriturismos, Calabria offers an intimate and personal experience that leaves a lasting impression.

Calabria's rich history and cultural heritage are also a significant draw for travelers seeking a deeper understanding of Italy's past. The region's strategic location has made it a crossroads of civilizations throughout history, resulting in a fascinating blend of influences. Explore the archaeological sites and museums to uncover the remnants of Magna Graecia, where ancient Greek colonies once thrived. Marvel at the Byzantine-influenced architecture that adorns churches and monasteries, offering a glimpse into the region's artistic and religious legacy.

Furthermore, Calabria's proximity to the sea has shaped its culinary traditions, giving rise to a gastronomic paradise for food enthusiasts. From farm-to-table experiences to vineyard visits, the region offers a wealth of culinary delights. Indulge in the flavors of traditional Calabrian dishes, such as spicy 'Nduja sausage, succulent swordfish, and the famous red onion of Tropea. Sample local wines, such as Cirò and Greco di Bianco, which perfectly complement the region's rich cuisine. By savoring Calabria's culinary offerings, you'll gain a deeper appreciation for its culture and traditions.

In Calabria, you have the opportunity to immerse yourself in a genuine Italian experience, free from the hustle and bustle of tourist crowds. This unspoiled region invites you to explore its hidden treasures, connect with its welcoming locals, and create lasting memories. Calabria is a destination that rewards those who seek the road less traveled, offering an authentic and enchanting journey through Italy's cultural and natural wonders.

Getting to Know the Region

Calabria, situated on the southernmost tip of the Italian peninsula, is a region of remarkable geographical and cultural significance. Its strategic location, nestled between the Tyrrhenian and Ionian Seas, has played a pivotal role in shaping its captivating history and diverse cultural heritage. From ancient times to the present day, Calabria has served as a crossroads where different civilizations have converged, leaving an indelible mark on its identity.

The geographical landscape of Calabria is characterized by its dramatic beauty. Majestic mountain ranges, verdant valleys, and crystalline coastlines paint a picturesque canvas that captivates visitors. The rugged Apennine Mountains traverse the region, with peaks reaching impressive heights and offering breathtaking panoramas. Among the notable ranges are the Sila and Aspromonte Mountains, each with their own unique ecosystems, wildlife, and hiking opportunities.

Calabria's coastlines, caressed by the Tyrrhenian and Ionian Seas, are adorned with pristine beaches, secluded coves, and charming fishing villages. The Tyrrhenian Coastline on the western side boasts sandy shores and picturesque seaside towns like Tropea and Pizzo, where visitors can relax on sun-drenched beaches and explore historical landmarks. On the eastern side, the Ionian Coastline boasts azure waters and enchanting spots such as Capo Vaticano and Soverato, ideal for water sports enthusiasts and beach lovers.

Beyond its natural splendors, Calabria's history is a testament to its cross-cultural encounters. Over the centuries, the region has been inhabited and influenced by various civilizations, including the Greeks, Romans, Byzantines, Normans, and Spanish, among others. Each era has contributed to the rich tapestry of Calabrian culture, leaving behind architectural treasures, archaeological sites, and artistic legacies that continue to captivate visitors today.

Exploring Calabria's historical sites is like stepping back in time. Ancient ruins such as the archaeological site of Locri Epizephyrii, an ancient Greek colony, and the Roman Theater of Reggio Calabria provide glimpses into the region's ancient past. The Byzantine influence is evident in architectural marvels like the Cattolica di Stilo, a Byzantine-style church perched atop a hill, and the Roccelletta di Borgia, a Byzantine fortress.

The convergence of cultures in Calabria is also reflected in its gastronomy. Calabrian cuisine is a delightful fusion of flavors, combining traditional Italian elements with Mediterranean and Middle Eastern influences. The region is renowned for its vibrant and spicy dishes, often featuring local ingredients such as 'nduja (spicy spreadable salami), bergamot fruit, and Calabrian chili peppers. Exploring the local markets and participating in food festivals offers an opportunity to savor the authentic tastes and aromas that define Calabrian culinary traditions.

Furthermore, Calabria's strategic location as a gateway between Italy and the Mediterranean has endowed it with a fascinating history of trade, conquest, and cultural exchange. The region's position made it an attractive destination for ancient seafarers, merchants, and explorers, resulting in a vibrant exchange of ideas, customs, and goods.

During the Greek colonization period, Calabria, known as Magna Graecia, became home to prosperous Greek city-states such as Locri Epizephyrii, Sybaris, and Kroton. These settlements thrived as centers of trade, art, and philosophy, leaving behind remarkable archaeological remnants that bear witness to the splendor of ancient Greek civilization.

As the Roman Empire expanded its dominion, Calabria became an integral part of the Roman Republic and later the Roman Empire. The Romans recognized the strategic value of Calabria's ports and natural resources, leading to the development of prosperous cities like Regium (present-day Reggio Calabria) and Rhegium Julium (now known as Reggio di Calabria). Roman ruins, such as thermal baths, amphitheaters, and aqueducts, can still be admired in various parts of the region.

The Byzantine Empire also left an indelible mark on Calabria's cultural landscape. In the wake of the Roman Empire's decline, Byzantine forces established control over the region, introducing Byzantine art, architecture, and religion. Calabria's villages and towns bear witness to this Byzantine heritage, with exquisite churches adorned with intricate frescoes and iconic religious icons.

Calabria's history continued to be shaped by subsequent invasions and occupations. The Normans, under the leadership of Robert Guiscard, conquered the region in the 11th century, blending their influence with the existing Byzantine and Lombard cultures. Norman castles and fortresses, such as the imposing Castello Svevo in Cosenza, stand as reminders of this period.

In later centuries, Calabria came under Spanish rule, contributing to the region's rich cultural tapestry. Spanish architecture and customs influenced various aspects of Calabrian life, leaving an imprint on the region's traditions, cuisine, and language.

Today, Calabria embraces its multifaceted heritage, celebrating its historical legacy through festivals, events, and the preservation of its architectural and artistic treasures. Travelers can explore ancient archaeological sites, stroll through medieval streets, and engage with local communities to gain a deeper understanding of Calabria's complex history.

As you embark on your journey through Calabria, the merging of cultures, the echoes of ancient civilizations, and the spirit of exploration will surround you. Calabria's geographical and cultural significance make it a captivating destination for those seeking to immerse themselves in the rich tapestry of Italy's hidden gem.

Chapter 1: Calabria at a Glance

In this chapter, we will provide an overview of Calabria, a region in southern Italy that is often referred to as the country's hidden gem. From its stunning coastlines to its rich cultural heritage, Calabria offers a unique and enchanting travel experience. We will delve into the geographical features, climate, and cultural background that make Calabria a must-visit destination.

Overview of Calabria:

Calabria is a region located in the "toe" of Italy's boot-shaped peninsula, nestled between the Ionian and Tyrrhenian Seas. This strategic position grants Calabria a remarkable coastline that stretches for hundreds of kilometers, offering breathtaking views and access to pristine beaches.

The geography of Calabria is characterized by its diverse and captivating natural beauty. Inland, the region is dominated by rugged mountains, including the Pollino and Sila ranges, which create a majestic backdrop. These mountains not only provide awe-inspiring vistas but also offer opportunities for outdoor activities such as hiking, skiing, and wildlife spotting. The Sila National Park, for instance, encompasses vast forests, serene lakes, and picturesque villages, showcasing the region's unspoiled wilderness.

Interwoven with the mountains are fertile valleys and plains, where agriculture thrives. Calabria is known for its production of citrus fruits, olives, vineyards, and an array of other agricultural products. These fertile lands yield high-quality ingredients that contribute to the region's renowned culinary traditions.

One of Calabria's most remarkable features is its stunning coastline. The Ionian and Tyrrhenian Seas embrace the region, offering crystal-clear waters and picturesque beaches. Along the Ionian Coastline, visitors can discover stretches of soft golden sand and hidden coves framed by dramatic cliffs. On the Tyrrhenian Coastline, charming seaside towns dot the landscape, inviting travelers to explore their narrow streets, taste local delicacies, and relax on sun-drenched shores. The coastline of Calabria is a paradise for beach lovers and water enthusiasts, providing opportunities for swimming, snorkeling, and sailing.

Beyond the coastal allure, Calabria is home to numerous charming villages and towns, each with its own unique character. These settlements showcase the region's rich history and cultural heritage, with influences from ancient Greek, Roman, Byzantine, and Norman civilizations. Walking through the streets of villages like Tropea, Gerace, or Stilo, travelers can admire medieval architecture, visit historic churches, and immerse themselves in the local way of life.

Additionally, Calabria's geographical location contributes to its unique climate. The region enjoys a Mediterranean climate, characterized by hot, dry summers and mild, wet winters. The coastal areas benefit from the moderating influence of the sea, resulting in pleasant temperatures and refreshing sea breezes during the summer months. Inland, the mountainous terrain brings cooler temperatures and occasional snowfall during the winter season, creating opportunities for winter sports enthusiasts.

The combination of Calabria's varied geography and favorable climate provides a haven for outdoor enthusiasts and nature lovers. Adventurers can embark on thrilling hikes through the mountains, exploring trails that lead to hidden waterfalls, panoramic viewpoints, and ancient ruins. The Sila National Park, with its extensive network of trails, offers opportunities for nature walks, birdwatching, and encounters with the region's unique flora and fauna.

For those seeking relaxation and rejuvenation, Calabria's pristine beaches beckon. The coastline is dotted with inviting beach resorts, where visitors can bask in the sun, swim in the azure waters, and indulge in the renowned Italian concept of "dolce far niente" - the sweetness of doing nothing. The beaches range from popular and bustling to secluded and tranquil, ensuring there is a perfect spot for every traveler's preference.

Beyond its natural beauty, Calabria's geography has played a significant role in shaping its culture and history. The region has been a crossroads of civilizations throughout the centuries, with various cultures leaving their marks on its architecture, traditions, and cuisine. The influence of ancient Greek colonies is evident in archaeological sites such as Locri Epizephiri and the ancient theater of Sibari, showcasing the region's rich historical legacy.

Furthermore, Calabria's fertile valleys and agricultural landscapes have shaped its culinary traditions. The region is renowned for its vibrant and flavorful cuisine, featuring dishes prepared with locally sourced ingredients such as olive oil, Calabrian chili peppers, and fresh seafood. Traditional specialties like 'nduja (a spicy spreadable salami), pasta alla Norma, and tartufo (a delicious ice cream dessert) highlight the region's culinary prowess.

In conclusion, Calabria's geography, encompassing rugged mountains, fertile valleys, and a picturesque coastline, offers a diverse and captivating natural environment. The region's climate and abundant natural resources contribute to a range of outdoor activities, from hiking and skiing to sunbathing and swimming. Calabria's geographical features have also left an indelible mark on its cultural heritage, from its historical sites to its renowned cuisine. With its splendid landscapes and rich cultural tapestry, Calabria entices travelers with an unforgettable experience that combines natural beauty, history, and culinary delights.

Geographical Features:

The geography of Calabria is incredibly diverse, encompassing a harmonious blend of mountains, hills, and coastal plains that captivate travelers with their beauty and variety. The region is dominated by the Apennine Mountain Range, which stretches across its center and contributes to its striking landscapes.

The Apennine Mountains in Calabria offer breathtaking vistas that are sure to leave visitors in awe. The peaks reach impressive heights, and their majestic presence creates a dramatic backdrop against the sky. As you explore the mountainous terrain, you'll be rewarded with panoramic views of rolling hills, deep valleys, and charming villages nestled in the slopes.

One of the remarkable features of the Calabrian mountains is the lushness of their forests. Dense vegetation covers the slopes, creating a green paradise where a diverse array of plant species thrives. The forests are home to towering trees, including oak, chestnut, and beech, which provide shelter to an abundance of wildlife.

Calabria's mountainous terrain is a haven for outdoor enthusiasts and adventurers. Hiking trails crisscross the landscape, offering opportunities to explore the region's hidden gems on foot. Whether you're a seasoned hiker or a casual nature lover, there are trails suitable for all skill levels, ranging from gentle paths that wind through picturesque valleys to challenging routes that lead to breathtaking summits.

During the winter months, the mountains of Calabria transform into a winter wonderland, attracting skiing and snowboarding enthusiasts. The region is home to several ski resorts, such as Camigliatello Silano and Gambarie, where you can glide down snow-covered slopes and indulge in winter sports.

The mountainous terrain of Calabria also provides an ideal habitat for a diverse range of wildlife. As you venture through the forests and traverse the rugged landscapes, keep an eye out for the native fauna that calls this region home. Deer, wild boar, foxes, and various bird species can often be spotted in their natural habitats, offering glimpses of the untamed beauty of Calabria's wilderness.

The mountains of Calabria not only provide opportunities for outdoor activities but also hold a deep cultural significance. They have served as a natural barrier, shaping the history and development of the region. The rugged terrain offered protection to ancient settlements, allowing them to flourish and preserve their unique traditions and way of life.

Calabria's mountains are not just a playground for adventurers but also an invitation to explore the region's rich history and cultural heritage. Scattered throughout the mountainous landscape, you will find ancient ruins, monasteries, and hermitages that bear witness to the region's past. These historic sites offer glimpses into the lives of past civilizations and provide a fascinating journey through time.

For those seeking tranquility and a connection with nature, the mountains of Calabria are the perfect retreat. The serene atmosphere, fresh mountain air, and the absence of city noise create an environment that encourages relaxation and rejuvenation. Whether you're meditating amidst the peaceful surroundings, enjoying a picnic with panoramic views, or simply taking a leisurely stroll along a forest trail, the mountains of Calabria offer a sanctuary away from the hustle and bustle of daily life.

Beyond the Apennine Mountains, Calabria's geography also encompasses picturesque hills and fertile plains. The rolling hills, adorned with vineyards, olive groves, and citrus orchards, paint a vibrant tapestry across the landscape. These agricultural areas not only contribute to the region's economy but also provide an enchanting backdrop for exploration and leisurely drives through scenic countryside.

Moving towards the coastline, Calabria's geography transitions into coastal plains that border the Ionian and Tyrrhenian Seas. The coastal areas are blessed with stunning beaches, hidden coves, and crystal-clear waters, making them ideal for sunbathing, swimming, and water sports. Calabria's coastline is often referred to as the "Coast of the Gods" due to its breathtaking beauty and mythical charm.

In conclusion, Calabria's geography encompasses a diverse range of landscapes, including mountains, hills, and coastal plains. The Apennine Mountains dominate the region, offering spectacular vistas, lush forests, and opportunities for outdoor activities. The hills and plains add their own charm, with vineyards, orchards, and scenic countryside. Together, these geographical features create a captivating and varied environment that beckons travelers to explore, discover, and connect with the natural and cultural wonders of Calabria.

Climate and Best Time to Visit:

Calabria enjoys a Mediterranean climate, characterized by mild winters and hot summers, making it an ideal destination for travelers seeking sun and warmth. The region is blessed with abundant sunshine throughout the year, creating a welcoming and inviting atmosphere for visitors.

During the winter months, from December to February, Calabria experiences mild temperatures, with average highs ranging from 10°C to 15°C (50°F to 59°F). While it may not be the peak tourist season, this time of year offers a tranquil and peaceful ambiance. The landscapes are adorned with lush greenery, and the historic towns and cultural sites are less crowded, allowing for a more intimate exploration of Calabria's treasures.

As spring emerges in March and extends through May, Calabria begins to bloom with vibrant colors and renewed energy. The temperatures start to rise, ranging from 15°C to 20°C (59°F to 68°F), creating pleasant conditions for outdoor activities and sightseeing. Springtime in Calabria is a perfect season for nature enthusiasts, as the countryside comes alive with blossoming flowers, and the national parks offer excellent opportunities for hiking, wildlife spotting, and enjoying the picturesque landscapes.

The summer season, from June to August, is the peak tourist period in Calabria. The temperatures soar, averaging around 30°C to 35°C (86°F to 95°F), attracting beach lovers and those seeking a lively atmosphere. Calabria's stunning coastline beckons with crystal-clear waters, inviting beaches, and a wide array of water sports and activities. The coastal towns and resorts buzz with energy, and the streets come alive with festivals, music, and cultural events. Summer is the ideal time to bask in the Mediterranean sun, indulge in delicious seafood, and immerse yourself in the vibrant ambiance of Calabria's coastal towns.

As the summer transitions into autumn, from September to November, Calabria experiences a gentle cool down. The temperatures range from 20°C to 25°C (68°F to 77°F), offering a comfortable climate for exploring both the coast and the inland areas. Autumn brings a sense of tranquility to Calabria, with fewer crowds and milder temperatures. It's a great time to visit the historic towns, delve into the region's cultural heritage, and indulge in the delectable flavors of the local cuisine.

Additionally, it's worth noting that Calabria's diverse geography contributes to microclimates within the region. Coastal areas benefit from the refreshing sea breeze, providing a pleasant respite from the summer heat. Inland areas, especially those nestled in the mountains, tend to be slightly cooler, offering a cool escape from the scorching temperatures during the peak of summer.

If you're a beach enthusiast, the summer months of June, July, and August are the prime time to explore Calabria's magnificent coastline. You can soak up the sun on the golden sandy beaches, swim in the crystal-clear waters of the Ionian and Tyrrhenian Seas, and engage in a variety of water activities like snorkeling, diving, and sailing. The beach resorts and beach clubs come to life, offering lively entertainment, beachfront dining, and a vibrant social scene.

For those who prefer a more relaxed and less crowded experience, spring (April to May) and autumn (September to October) are ideal. During these seasons, the temperatures are mild, ranging from 15°C to 25°C (59°F to 77°F), allowing for comfortable exploration of Calabria's historical sites, charming villages, and natural wonders. You can enjoy leisurely walks along the coastal promenades, visit ancient ruins without the hustle and bustle of peak tourist periods, and savor the tranquility of Calabria's countryside.

Winter in Calabria offers a unique charm, particularly for travelers who appreciate a peaceful ambiance and off-season experiences. While the temperatures are cooler, ranging from 10°C to 15°C (50°F to 59°F), Calabria's historical landmarks and cultural attractions remain open, providing a quieter and more intimate setting to delve into the region's rich heritage. You can wander through medieval towns, visit museums and art galleries, and engage with the friendly locals who warmly welcome visitors year-round.

Ultimately, the best time to visit Calabria depends on your personal preferences and the type of experience you seek. Whether you're drawn to the lively atmosphere of summer, the milder temperatures of spring and autumn, or the tranquility of winter, Calabria offers a remarkable journey through its captivating landscapes, rich history, and warm hospitality.

Cultural Background and Influences:

Calabria's rich cultural heritage is a testament to its historical significance and the diverse civilizations that have shaped its identity over time. The region's strategic location made it a desirable territory for various ancient civilizations, including the Greeks, Romans, and Byzantines. Each of these cultures left an indelible mark on Calabria, contributing to its unique blend of traditions, architecture, and artistic expressions.

The Greeks were among the earliest settlers in Calabria, establishing colonies along the coast during the 8th and 7th centuries BCE. Their influence is evident in the archaeological sites that dot the landscape, such as the ancient city of Locri Epizephiri, which features well-preserved ruins, including temples, amphitheaters, and mosaics. These ancient Greek settlements played a vital role in the cultural and economic development of the region, leaving behind a legacy of art, philosophy, and literature.

During the Roman era, Calabria became an important part of the Roman Empire. Magna Graecia, the name given to the Greek colonies in Southern Italy, was gradually assimilated into the Roman culture. Roman ruins can be found throughout the region, including the well-preserved remains of the ancient city of Rhegion (modern-day Reggio Calabria), which showcases impressive structures like the Roman Baths and the Aragonese Castle. The Romans also introduced their architectural and engineering expertise, leaving behind aqueducts, amphitheaters, and road systems that served as the backbone of their empire.

With the decline of the Roman Empire, Calabria came under Byzantine rule in the 6th century CE. The Byzantines, who were known for their Byzantine art and architecture, left an enduring legacy in Calabria. Byzantine influences can be seen in the religious art and frescoes found in churches and monasteries, such as the Byzantine-style Cattolica di Stilo, an iconic church perched on a hilltop.

Beyond the influence of ancient civilizations, the local culture of Calabria is shaped by the vibrant traditions and customs of its people. The Calabrian population, known for their warmth, hospitality, and strong sense of community, takes pride in preserving and celebrating their heritage.

Traditional festivals and events showcase various aspects of Calabrian culture, including music, dance, folk costumes, and culinary specialties.

Whether it's participating in the lively Tarantella dance, savoring traditional Calabrian dishes like 'nduja (spicy spreadable salami) and homemade pasta, or witnessing the passionate devotion during religious processions, visitors to Calabria are immersed in a living tapestry of cultural expressions.

In addition to the tangible remnants of its past, Calabria's cultural heritage is also embodied in the intangible aspects of everyday life, such as dialects, proverbs, and family values that have been passed down through generations. These intangible cultural elements contribute to the sense of identity and pride that resonates among the Calabrian people.

Moreover, Calabria's cultural heritage extends beyond the realms of ancient civilizations and local traditions. The region has also been influenced by the interactions with neighboring cultures and the waves of migration throughout history. These external influences have further enriched the cultural fabric of Calabria, adding layers of diversity and creating a fusion of customs and practices.

One notable influence on Calabrian culture is the Norman period, which began in the 11th century when the Normans conquered southern Italy. The Normans brought with them their own architectural style, language, and feudal system, leaving an architectural legacy that can be seen in the impressive Norman castles and fortifications that still stand today. These structures, such as the Castle of Cosenza and the Castle of Corigliano Calabro, offer a glimpse into Calabria's medieval past.

In more recent history, Calabria experienced significant waves of emigration, particularly during the late 19th and early 20th centuries. Calabrians sought opportunities and a better life abroad, primarily in North and South America. This emigration had a profound impact on the region's culture, as Calabrian traditions and customs spread to distant shores, creating vibrant diaspora communities that maintained strong connections with their homeland. Today, Calabrian communities around the world celebrate their heritage through festivals, language preservation, and cultural associations.

In the realm of gastronomy, Calabria's culinary traditions showcase the fusion of influences that have shaped the region's cuisine. Greek, Roman, Byzantine, Arab, and Spanish flavors all find their place on the Calabrian table. The use of local ingredients, such as Calabrian chili peppers, 'nduja, bergamot, and Tropea onions, creates a distinct and flavorful cuisine that reflects the region's agricultural abundance and historical ties.

The cultural heritage of Calabria is not confined to the past but is an integral part of daily life in the region. It can be experienced through interactions with locals, exploring traditional crafts like pottery and weaving, or participating in age-old festivals that bring communities together in celebration. The warmth and hospitality of the Calabrian people are evident in their embrace of visitors, as they eagerly share their customs, stories, and local treasures.

Ultimately, Calabria's rich cultural heritage is an invitation to delve deeper, beyond the surface attractions, and discover the hidden layers of history, traditions, and influences that have shaped this captivating region. It is an opportunity to witness firsthand the resilience, pride, and passion that the people of Calabria possess in preserving and showcasing their unique identity.

As you embark on your journey through Calabria, prepare to immerse yourself in a unique blend of history, nature, and authentic Italian culture. This chapter sets the stage for the exploration that lies ahead, providing essential context and insights into the allure of Calabria's hidden wonders.

Chapter 2: Exploring Calabria's Coastal Marvels

The Tyrrhenian Coastline

The Tyrrhenian Coastline of Calabria is a treasure trove of coastal marvels, each offering its own unique charm and allure. From stunning beaches and seaside towns to a wide range of water sports and activities, as well as charming coastal villages, there is something for everyone along this picturesque stretch of coastline. Let's delve into six of Calabria's coastal marvels on the Tyrrhenian Coastline:

Tropea:
Tropea, the "Jewel of the Tyrrhenian Sea," is a coastal paradise that effortlessly combines breathtaking natural beauty with a rich historical and cultural heritage. This captivating seaside town, perched on a cliff overlooking the azure waters below, casts a spell on all who visit.

The picturesque beach of Tropea is a true gem, with its soft golden sands and crystal-clear waters. As you step onto the shore, you'll be mesmerized by the stunning panoramic views of the Tyrrhenian Sea stretching out before you. The gentle waves invite you for a refreshing swim or a leisurely dip, while the warm sun casts a golden glow over the entire coastline.

But Tropea is not only about its stunning beach. The town's historic center, characterized by its charming old town, beckons you to wander through its narrow cobblestone streets and immerse yourself in its timeless atmosphere. Each step reveals a new delight, from ancient buildings adorned with colorful flowers to hidden squares bustling with local life.

Make sure to visit the historic Tropea Cathedral, a magnificent structure that stands proudly as a symbol of the town's religious and architectural heritage. Step inside to marvel at its ornate interior, adorned with exquisite frescoes and religious artifacts. From the cathedral's vantage point, you'll enjoy sweeping views of the town and the shimmering sea beyond.

As you explore Tropea, you'll quickly discover the town's culinary pride: the famous red onions. Known as "Cipolla Rossa di Tropea" in Italian, these sweet and flavorful onions are a local specialty. You'll find them incorporated into various traditional dishes, adding a unique touch to the region's gastronomic offerings. Don't miss the opportunity to sample the local cuisine and savor the distinctive flavors that these onions bring to the table.

Beyond its natural and cultural attractions, Tropea offers a vibrant atmosphere with its lively squares, charming boutiques, and inviting cafés. Take a leisurely stroll along the promenade, browse through artisan shops for unique souvenirs, or simply find a cozy spot to sit and soak up the vibrant ambiance of this coastal gem.

In addition to its natural beauty and rich history, Tropea offers a range of activities and experiences that further enhance its appeal as a captivating seaside destination.

For those seeking adventure, Tropea is an excellent base for exploring the surrounding waters. Embark on a boat tour and venture to the nearby Aeolian Islands, a volcanic archipelago known for its stunning landscapes and pristine beaches. Dive into the crystalline waters and discover a vibrant underwater world teeming with colorful marine life. Snorkeling and scuba diving enthusiasts will be thrilled by the opportunity to explore the hidden treasures beneath the surface.

Back on land, Tropea's surrounding countryside provides ample opportunities for exploration. Take a leisurely hike along the rugged coastal trails, where breathtaking panoramic views await at every turn. Explore the countryside dotted with vineyards and olive groves, and savor the flavors of the region through wine tasting and olive oil sampling experiences.

Food lovers will be delighted by the culinary offerings in Tropea. Indulge in the local cuisine, which highlights the bounty of the sea and the region's agricultural heritage. Savor freshly caught seafood dishes, such as grilled swordfish or marinated anchovies, accompanied by locally grown produce and traditional Calabrian flavors. Be sure to pair your meal with a glass of local wine, such as the renowned Cirò, produced in the nearby vineyards.

As the sun begins to set, Tropea takes on a magical ambiance. The town's cliffside location offers unforgettable sunset vistas, painting the sky with hues of pink, orange, and gold. Find a cozy spot on a terrace or along the promenade to witness the spectacle and capture the perfect photograph to commemorate your visit.

In the evening, Tropea comes alive with a vibrant nightlife scene. Discover lively bars and restaurants offering live music, traditional folk performances, and a warm, welcoming atmosphere. Join in the festivities and mingle with locals and fellow travelers, creating memories and forging connections that will last a lifetime.

Tropea truly encompasses the essence of a dreamy seaside getaway. Its combination of natural beauty, rich history, enticing cuisine, and warm hospitality make it a destination that lingers in the hearts of those fortunate enough to experience it. Whether you're seeking relaxation, exploration, or cultural immersion, Tropea promises an unforgettable journey along the Tyrrhenian Coastline of Calabria.

Capo Vaticano:

Capo Vaticano, a coastal gem located in close proximity to Tropea, is a true paradise for beach lovers. This enchanting destination on the Tyrrhenian Coastline is celebrated for its breathtaking cliffs, secluded coves, and pristine white sandy beaches, making it a must-visit for those seeking natural beauty and tranquility.

As you arrive at Capo Vaticano, you'll be immediately captivated by the dramatic cliffs that overlook the crystal-clear turquoise waters below. These majestic cliffs create a stunning backdrop for the picturesque beaches that await your exploration. The soft, powdery white sand invites you to sink your toes into its warmth and provides the perfect spot to lay down your beach towel and bask in the Mediterranean sun.

The beaches of Capo Vaticano offer more than just a place to relax and soak up the sun. The tranquil and transparent waters beckon you for a refreshing swim. Immerse yourself in the pristine turquoise sea and experience the sensation of weightlessness as you float in its gentle embrace. Snorkelers will find themselves immersed in a vibrant underwater world, with colorful fish and marine life thriving amidst the rocky outcrops and coral formations.

For those seeking a touch of adventure, Capo Vaticano offers the opportunity to embark on a boat trip to explore the hidden treasures of the coastline. Sail along the azure waters and discover secret caves and secluded bays that are inaccessible by land. Marvel at the natural rock formations and the interplay of light and shadow that creates a mesmerizing atmosphere. Whether you choose to explore these wonders by kayak, paddleboard, or on a guided boat tour, the experience will undoubtedly leave you in awe of the coastal splendor.

Capo Vaticano is not just a destination for beachgoers; it is a place where nature's beauty unfolds in all its glory. The surrounding cliffs, covered in lush Mediterranean vegetation, offer scenic hiking trails that lead to breathtaking viewpoints overlooking the sea. Take a leisurely stroll along the coastal paths and immerse yourself in the sights, sounds, and scents of this unspoiled natural landscape.

As the sun sets over Capo Vaticano, casting a golden glow across the horizon, you'll realize that this coastal paradise is a place where time seems to stand still. It's a place where you can let go of your worries, embrace the serenity of the surroundings, and reconnect with nature.

The allure of Capo Vaticano extends beyond its natural beauty. The region is also renowned for its warm hospitality and charming coastal atmosphere. Along the shoreline, you'll find a selection of beachside cafes, restaurants, and bars, offering delicious local cuisine and refreshing drinks. Indulge in the flavors of Calabria, savoring fresh seafood dishes, mouthwatering pasta, and locally produced wines.

As you explore the beaches of Capo Vaticano, you'll discover a sense of tranquility and seclusion that allows you to truly unwind and escape the pressures of daily life. The hidden coves, tucked away between the cliffs, provide a sense of privacy, making them perfect for those seeking a peaceful retreat. Find your own little slice of paradise, where you can relax, read a book, or simply listen to the gentle lapping of the waves.

For the more adventurous travelers, Capo Vaticano offers opportunities for outdoor activities beyond the beach. The rugged cliffs and lush surroundings provide an ideal setting for hiking and exploring the coastal trails. Follow the winding paths that lead you through fragrant pine forests, past breathtaking viewpoints, and towards hidden coves that can only be reached on foot. The combination of nature, adventure, and stunning landscapes makes Capo Vaticano a haven for outdoor enthusiasts.

While the beaches of Capo Vaticano are undeniably the highlight, the area also boasts cultural and historical attractions. Visit the nearby town of Ricadi, with its charming streets and traditional architecture, and discover the local traditions and heritage of Calabria. Explore the ancient ruins of the Torre Marrana, a watchtower dating back to the Norman era, and gain insight into the region's fascinating past.

In Capo Vaticano, time seems to lose its meaning as you immerse yourself in the beauty of nature and the peaceful rhythm of coastal life. Whether you're seeking relaxation, adventure, or a blend of both, this coastal gem offers an idyllic retreat where you can create lasting memories and find solace in the simple pleasures of sun, sea, and sand.

Capo Vaticano is a testament to the natural wonders that Calabria has to offer, and it invites you to experience a slice of paradise on the Tyrrhenian Coastline. Allow yourself to be swept away by the beauty of its cliffs, the tranquility of its beaches, and the warmth of its hospitality. Let Capo Vaticano be your sanctuary, where you can disconnect from the outside world and reconnect with yourself and the wonders of nature.

Pizzo:
Amalfi, often regarded as the crown jewel of the Amalfi Coast, is a picturesque town with a rich historical heritage. Nestled amidst rugged cliffs and azure waters, this enchanting destination captures the essence of Italian coastal charm. In this section, we will delve into the historical background of Amalfi, explore its top attractions, and provide insights on how to make the most of your time in Amalfi Town.

Historical Background

Amalfi boasts a captivating history that dates back to the 9th century when it emerged as a powerful maritime republic. As a maritime powerhouse, Amalfi had extensive trade connections with the Byzantine Empire and played a significant role in the Mediterranean trade routes. Its maritime code, known as the "Tabula Amalphitana," became the basis for maritime laws across Europe.

The town's prosperity during the medieval period is evident in its impressive architecture, which showcases a blend of Arabic, Byzantine, and Norman influences. Amalfi's historic center, recognized as a UNESCO World Heritage Site, is a treasure trove of ancient buildings, narrow alleyways, and charming piazzas.

Top Attractions

Amalfi offers a range of attractions that are sure to captivate visitors. Here are some of the must-visit sights in Amalfi:

Amalfi Cathedral (Duomo di Amalfi): This magnificent cathedral stands as a symbol of Amalfi's grandeur. Admire its impressive medieval facade, climb the grand staircase, and explore the ornate interior adorned with Byzantine mosaics and relics.

Cloister of Paradise (Chiostro del Paradiso): Located next to the cathedral, this serene cloister showcases beautiful Arab-Norman architecture. Take a leisurely stroll among the columns adorned with intricate designs and enjoy the peaceful atmosphere.

Museo della Carta (Museum of Paper): Discover the fascinating history of paper production in Amalfi at this museum. Learn about the techniques used in handmade paper production and view ancient paper-making tools and equipment.

Valle delle Ferriere: For nature enthusiasts, a visit to Valle delle Ferriere is a must. This lush nature reserve offers scenic hiking trails, waterfalls, and a diverse array of flora and fauna. Immerse yourself in the natural beauty of the Amalfi Coast.

Exploring Amalfi Town

Amalfi Town itself is a charming destination to explore. Start by wandering through the labyrinthine streets of the historic center, taking in the vibrant atmosphere and admiring the traditional pastel-colored houses. Visit the local shops to browse for handmade ceramics, limoncello, and other regional specialties.

Stroll along the bustling harbor promenade and soak in the views of the sparkling Mediterranean Sea. Consider taking a boat tour or hiring a private boat to explore the coastline from a different perspective.

Indulge in the local cuisine at one of the many trattorias and restaurants in town. Sample fresh seafood dishes, traditional pasta, and regional delicacies like sfogliatelle (a flaky pastry filled with sweet ricotta) or gelato made with locally grown lemons.

To fully immerse yourself in the Amalfi experience, consider participating in a cooking class or wine tasting session to learn about the local culinary traditions and flavors.

Amalfi Town serves as an excellent base for further exploration of the Amalfi Coast, with its convenient location and accessibility to other nearby towns such as Positano, Ravello, and Sorrento. Take advantage of boat or bus services to venture out and discover more of the coastal beauty that awaits you.

Whether you're a history enthusiast, a nature lover, or a foodie, Amalfi Town offers a delightful blend of cultural heritage, natural splendor, and gastronomic delights that will leave you with unforgettable memories of your Amalfi Coast journey.Pizzo, a gem nestled on the picturesque coastline of the Tyrrhenian Sea, is a coastal town that effortlessly blends charm, history, and culinary delights. As you arrive in Pizzo, you'll be greeted by its enchanting atmosphere and a sense of stepping back in time.

The medieval streets of Pizzo's old town beckon you to explore their narrow, winding paths. Lose yourself in the maze of cobblestone streets lined with historic buildings, colorful houses, and charming local shops. Admire the architecture that reflects the town's rich history, from Gothic to Baroque influences. Discover hidden squares adorned with fountains and quaint cafes, where you can pause for a moment and soak in the ambiance of this ancient town.

One of the highlights of Pizzo is the imposing Pizzo Castle, which stands proudly atop a rocky promontory overlooking the sea. This well-preserved fortress dates back to the 15th century and offers panoramic views of the coastline. Take a leisurely stroll along the castle's ramparts and imagine the tales of the past that echo through its walls. The castle is a testament to Pizzo's historical significance and provides a glimpse into the town's maritime heritage.

No visit to Pizzo would be complete without indulging in its famous culinary delight, Tartufo di Pizzo. This delectable local ice cream treat is a mouthwatering combination of rich chocolate and creamy gelato, often filled with a surprise center of liqueur or fruit. Take a moment to savor the flavors as you sit in one of the charming gelaterias or cafés that line the streets. The Tartufo di Pizzo has gained international acclaim and is a true symbol of Pizzo's gastronomic excellence.

As you make your way to the beach at Pizzo, you'll be greeted by a tranquil oasis. The sandy shores provide a perfect setting for relaxation, sunbathing, and immersing yourself in the beauty of the surroundings. Find a comfortable spot on the beach, lay out your towel, and let the warm sun envelop you as you listen to the gentle lapping of the waves. Take in the panoramic views of the azure waters of the Tyrrhenian Sea and the dramatic coastline that stretches into the distance.

The beach at Pizzo offers a serene atmosphere that invites you to unwind and escape from the worries of everyday life.

Whether you choose to take a leisurely stroll along the shoreline, dip your toes in the refreshing waters, or simply bask in the sun's embrace, you'll find a sense of peace and tranquility that permeates the air.

As you continue your exploration of Pizzo, you'll discover that this charming coastal town has even more to offer beyond its historic streets and delightful ice cream. Immerse yourself in the local culture and experience the unique attractions that make Pizzo a must-visit destination.

One of the notable attractions in Pizzo is the Church of Piedigrotta, a remarkable underground church carved into the tufa rock. This hidden gem is adorned with intricate rock sculptures and stunning works of art, creating a mystical atmosphere. Explore the dimly lit chambers and marvel at the craftsmanship that went into creating this extraordinary place of worship.

For history enthusiasts, a visit to the Murat Castle is a must. Built in the 15th century, this castle holds significant historical importance as it was the place where Joachim Murat, King of Naples and brother-in-law of Napoleon Bonaparte, was captured and executed. Explore the castle's grounds, climb its towers, and soak in the panoramic views of the surrounding landscape and the sea.

To delve deeper into Pizzo's history, take a stroll along the picturesque Piazza della Repubblica, the heart of the old town. Admire the charming architecture and the beautiful fountain that takes center stage in the square. The piazza is a gathering place for locals and visitors alike, offering a vibrant atmosphere and a chance to observe the rhythm of daily life in Pizzo.

For those seeking a bit of adventure, consider taking a boat tour to explore the nearby caves and grottoes that dot the coastline. Marvel at the natural wonders carved by the sea over centuries and enjoy the breathtaking views of the rugged cliffs and crystal-clear waters. These boat tours provide a unique perspective of the coastline and allow you to appreciate the coastal beauty from a different vantage point.

As the day draws to a close, make your way back to Pizzo's beach to witness a spectacular sunset over the Tyrrhenian Sea. Find a comfortable spot on the sand or sit at a beachfront bar, sipping a refreshing drink as the sky transforms into a canvas of vibrant colors. The serene atmosphere combined with the awe-inspiring sunset creates a moment of pure tranquility and beauty that will remain etched in your memory.

Pizzo's rich history, cultural treasures, and breathtaking coastal beauty make it an enchanting destination along the Tyrrhenian Coastline. Whether you're wandering through its medieval streets, indulging in delectable treats, exploring its historical sites, or simply unwinding on its stunning beach, Pizzo promises an experience that will capture your heart and leave you yearning to return.

Scilla:
Scilla, often referred to as the "Venice of Calabria," is a coastal village that exudes a truly magical atmosphere. Nestled along the Tyrrhenian Coastline, Scilla offers a blend of natural beauty, historical charm, and a captivating ambiance that enchants visitors.

The ancient Ruffo Castle stands proudly as the iconic landmark of Scilla, perched on a rocky outcrop overlooking the shimmering waters of the Tyrrhenian Sea. This imposing fortress dates back centuries and provides a glimpse into the region's rich history. As you explore the castle, you'll be treated to panoramic views of the coastline, offering a breathtaking vista of the sea and the charming village below.

One of the highlights of Scilla is the enchanting fishing district of Chianalea. As you meander through its narrow streets, you'll be captivated by the sight of colorful houses that seemingly cascade down to the waterfront. These vibrant buildings, adorned with flowers and laundry hanging from the windows, create a picturesque and romantic setting. Immerse yourself in the atmosphere of this traditional fishing village as you discover quaint seafood restaurants, charming cafés, and local artisan shops that line the streets.
Scilla's beach is a tranquil escape, inviting you to relax and unwind in its serene surroundings. The beach offers soft golden sands and clear, inviting waters that beckon you for a refreshing swim. Whether you choose to bask in the sun on a beach towel, take a leisurely stroll along the shoreline, or engage in water activities such as snorkeling or paddleboarding, the beach at Scilla provides an idyllic setting to connect with nature and rejuvenate your senses.

While in Scilla, don't miss the opportunity to sample the local seafood delicacies. The village is renowned for its fresh catch, and you can indulge in delicious dishes that highlight the flavors of the sea. From traditional fish soups to grilled seafood platters, Scilla offers a gastronomic journey that will delight your taste buds.

As the sun sets over Scilla, the village takes on a magical ambiance. The soft glow of streetlights reflects on the calm waters, creating a romantic atmosphere that is perfect for a leisurely evening stroll. Take in the beauty of the illuminated castle, admire the reflections dancing on the sea's surface, and revel in the tranquility that envelops the village.

Scilla is a place where time seems to slow down, allowing you to fully embrace the charm of this coastal gem. Whether you are exploring the narrow streets of Chianalea, relaxing on the beach, or immersing yourself in the local culture and cuisine, Scilla offers a truly enchanting experience that will leave a lasting impression.

As you delve deeper into the enchanting village of Scilla, you'll discover that it holds even more treasures beyond its captivating castle, picturesque streets, and serene beach.

Take a leisurely stroll along the waterfront promenade, lined with quaint cafes and charming gelaterias. Savor a cup of espresso or indulge in a delicious gelato while enjoying the gentle sea breeze and panoramic views of the Tyrrhenian Sea. The promenade is a hub of activity, bustling with locals and visitors alike, creating a lively and vibrant atmosphere.

For a truly immersive experience, consider taking a boat excursion around Scilla. Board a traditional fishing boat and set sail along the coast, exploring hidden coves, dramatic cliffs, and sea caves. As you navigate the azure waters, you'll be treated to breathtaking vistas of Scilla's coastline, with its rugged beauty and untouched nature. This maritime adventure allows you to see Scilla from a different perspective, appreciating the village's charm from the sea.

If you're seeking a cultural encounter, pay a visit to the Church of Santa Maria di Porto Salvo. This beautiful church dates back to the 16th century and is a testament to Scilla's religious heritage. Admire the intricate architecture, ornate decorations, and the peaceful atmosphere that fills the sacred space.

Scilla is also known for its lively summer festivals, where locals come together to celebrate their traditions and showcase their vibrant culture. The most famous of these is the Feast of St. Rocco, held in August. During this event, the streets come alive with processions, music, dancing, and fireworks, creating an atmosphere of joy and unity. Immerse yourself in the festivities, mingle with the locals, and embrace the lively spirit that fills the air.

If you have time, consider venturing beyond the village of Scilla to explore the surrounding natural wonders. Nearby, you'll find the stunning Costa Viola, a stretch of coastline known for its dramatic cliffs and turquoise waters. Take a scenic drive along this picturesque coastal road, marveling at the breathtaking vistas and stopping at viewpoints to capture memorable photographs.

As your time in Scilla comes to an end, you'll carry with you the memories of its magical atmosphere, welcoming locals, and the sense of tranquility that permeates every corner. Scilla is a coastal marvel that combines history, natural beauty, and a vibrant cultural scene, making it a destination that truly captures the essence of Calabria's coastal charm.

Amantea:
Amantea, nestled between the majestic mountains and the sparkling sea, is a captivating town that offers a delightful blend of natural beauty and historical charm. As you arrive in Amantea, you'll be greeted by a long stretch of sandy beach that invites you to indulge in moments of relaxation and exhilarating water sports adventures.

The historic center of Amantea is a treasure trove of architectural wonders and cultural heritage. Take a leisurely stroll through the narrow streets, lined with charming old buildings adorned with vibrant flowers. Discover hidden alleyways that lead to quaint squares where locals gather for lively conversations. Immerse yourself in the town's rich history as you pass by centuries-old churches and palaces, each with its own story to tell.

A highlight of Amantea is the magnificent 16th-century Amantea Castle. Perched atop a hill, the castle offers a commanding view of the town and the glistening sea beyond. Step inside and wander through its grand halls, marveling at the ancient stone walls and intricate details that have withstood the test of time. From the castle's towers, you can soak in panoramic vistas of the coastline, where the azure waters meet the golden sands.

The promenade in Amantea is a perfect spot to enjoy the breathtaking views and embrace the refreshing sea breeze. Take a leisurely stroll along the palm-lined pathway, feeling the warmth of the sun on your skin and listening to the rhythmic sound of the waves crashing against the shore. The panoramic views of the coastline stretch out before you, creating a sense of serenity and awe-inspiring beauty.

Amantea's beach is a haven for beach lovers and water enthusiasts alike. The long sandy shore beckons you to lay down your towel, soak up the sun's rays, and indulge in moments of pure relaxation. The calm and inviting waters of the Tyrrhenian Sea are ideal for a refreshing swim, allowing you to cool off and embrace the coastal serenity. If you're seeking a more adventurous experience, Amantea offers opportunities for water sports such as sailing, windsurfing, and jet skiing, adding a thrilling dimension to your beach getaway.

Whether you choose to bask in the tranquility of the beach or embark on exciting water sports activities, Amantea offers a coastal experience that caters to every preference. The juxtaposition of the stunning natural scenery with the town's rich history creates an enchanting atmosphere that is sure to leave a lasting impression.

In Amantea, you'll find a perfect blend of relaxation, cultural exploration, and outdoor adventure. It's a place where you can unwind, immerse yourself in the local culture, and create cherished memories against the backdrop of the magnificent sea and majestic mountains. Amantea truly captures the essence of Calabria's coastal charm, leaving visitors with a sense of awe and a longing to return.

As the day transitions into evening, the enchantment of Amantea continues to unfold. The town comes alive with a vibrant atmosphere, and the enticing aromas of local cuisine waft through the air. Explore the charming streets of Amantea's historic center, and you'll discover a plethora of delightful cafes, trattorias, and restaurants serving up traditional Calabrian dishes.

Indulge in the flavors of the region as you savor freshly caught seafood, succulent meats, and locally grown produce. Don't miss the opportunity to try 'nduja, a spicy spreadable salami that is a signature of Calabrian cuisine. Pair your meal with a glass of locally produced wine, and allow your taste buds to be delighted by the authentic flavors of Amantea.

After a satisfying meal, take a leisurely stroll along the illuminated promenade, where the shimmering lights reflect on the calm waters of the Tyrrhenian Sea. The tranquil ambiance sets the stage for an unforgettable evening. Find a cozy spot at one of the seaside bars or gelaterias, and savor a delicious gelato or a refreshing cocktail as you soak in the captivating views.

For those seeking a deeper connection with nature, Amantea offers opportunities to explore the surrounding mountains. Lace up your hiking boots and embark on a scenic trail that winds through lush forests, revealing breathtaking vistas along the way. Marvel at the rugged beauty of the landscape, and breathe in the fresh mountain air as you immerse yourself in the serenity of nature.

As your time in Amantea draws to a close, the memories of its picturesque beaches, historical treasures, and warm hospitality will linger in your heart. The charm and tranquility of this coastal town will leave an indelible mark, beckoning you to return and continue your exploration of Calabria's coastal marvels.

Amantea is more than just a destination; it's an invitation to slow down, embrace the beauty of nature, savor delectable flavors, and immerse yourself in the rich history and culture of Calabria. It's a place where you can find a perfect balance between relaxation, adventure, and culinary delights, making it a truly remarkable coastal marvel along the Tyrrhenian Coastline.

Scalea:
Scalea is a hidden coastal gem nestled along the Tyrrhenian Coastline of Calabria. This picturesque town is blessed with rugged cliffs, hidden caves, and breathtaking sandy beaches, making it an ideal destination for those seeking both natural beauty and seaside relaxation.

As you arrive in Scalea, you'll be captivated by the dramatic landscape that surrounds it. The rugged cliffs that frame the coastline create a sense of grandeur, while the hidden caves beckon the adventurous to explore their mysterious depths. Take a leisurely stroll along the shoreline and let the sound of crashing waves against the cliffs create a symphony of nature that resonates deep within your soul.

The historic center of Scalea is a charming maze of narrow streets and ancient buildings that harken back to centuries past. Lose yourself in the labyrinthine alleys, where each turn reveals a hidden treasure waiting to be discovered. Admire the architectural beauty of the well-preserved buildings, some dating back to medieval times, and imagine the stories that they hold within their walls.

One of the standout attractions in Scalea is the Talao Tower, an impressive structure that stands as a sentinel overlooking the coastline. Climb to the top of this ancient tower and be rewarded with panoramic views that stretch as far as the eye can see. The sight of the azure waters merging with the golden sands is a sight to behold, evoking a sense of awe and wonder.

Scalea's beaches are a true paradise for sunseekers and water enthusiasts. The sandy shores invite you to bask in the warm Mediterranean sun, providing the perfect spot for lounging and relaxation. Whether you choose to lay out a beach towel and lose yourself in a book or take a refreshing dip in the clear, inviting waters, Scalea's beaches offer an idyllic setting for unwinding and rejuvenation.

For those with a sense of adventure, the waters of Scalea provide ample opportunities for snorkeling and diving. Don your snorkel and mask to explore the vibrant underwater world, where colorful fish and marine life dance among the submerged rocks and reefs. Dive deeper into the depths and discover hidden treasures, such as underwater caves and ancient shipwrecks, waiting to be explored.

Scalea truly embodies the essence of a coastal paradise, with its rugged beauty, rich history, and inviting beaches. Whether you seek serenity, adventure, or a blend of both, Scalea offers a slice of Calabrian coastal heaven. Embrace the tranquility of the cliffs, immerse yourself in the azure waters, and let Scalea weave its magic, leaving you with unforgettable memories of this coastal gem.

As the sun begins to set over Scalea, the town takes on a magical ambiance. The golden hues of the evening sky cast a warm glow over the cliffs and beaches, creating a serene atmosphere that is perfect for a romantic stroll along the waterfront. The sound of waves gently lapping against the shore sets a soothing rhythm as you meander hand in hand with your loved one, creating memories that will last a lifetime.

In addition to its natural beauty, Scalea is also known for its vibrant local culture and gastronomy. Explore the charming streets lined with quaint shops and traditional trattorias, where you can savor the flavors of Calabrian cuisine. Indulge in fresh seafood dishes, such as grilled swordfish or local specialties like 'nduja, a spicy spreadable salami that packs a flavorful punch. Pair your meal with a glass of local wine and savor the delightful combination of flavors that are a true reflection of the region's culinary heritage.

For history enthusiasts, Scalea offers a glimpse into the past through its archaeological sites and museums. Visit the Museum of Scalea, which houses a collection of artifacts that tell the story of the town's rich history, including ancient Roman and Greek artifacts. Explore the ruins of the nearby town of Laos, an ancient settlement that dates back to the 7th century BC, and imagine what life was like in this ancient civilization.

As your time in Scalea comes to an end, you'll carry with you the memories of its rugged cliffs, hidden caves, and beautiful beaches. The tranquility and natural beauty of this coastal gem will remain etched in your heart, serving as a reminder of the peaceful moments spent by the sea. Scalea invites you to immerse yourself in its captivating charm, offering a truly authentic experience of Calabria's coastal marvels.

These coastal marvels along the Tyrrhenian Coastline of Calabria offer a blend of natural beauty, historical significance, and a relaxed beachside atmosphere. Each destination has its own distinct character, inviting you to uncover the wonders of Calabria's coastal treasures.

The Ionian Coastline

The Ionian Coastline of Calabria is home to several coastal marvels that will leave you enchanted. These destinations offer a diverse range of experiences, from pristine beaches to historical landmarks, allowing you to discover the unique allure of this coastal region. Here are six coastal marvels along the Ionian Coastline that are worth exploring:

Capo Rizzuto:
Capo Rizzuto, nestled along the Ionian Coastline, truly stands out as a coastal gem that showcases the best of Calabria's natural beauty. This enchanting destination boasts long stretches of sandy beaches and tranquil waters, offering a haven of relaxation and serenity.

As you set foot on the shores of Capo Rizzuto, you'll immediately feel a sense of calm wash over you. The serene ambiance creates an atmosphere of peace and tranquility, making it the perfect escape from the hustle and bustle of everyday life. The gentle sounds of the waves lapping against the shore and the soothing sea breeze dancing through the air create a symphony of nature's melody, further enhancing the sense of serenity that envelops the coastline.

Take leisurely walks along the coastline, allowing your feet to sink into the soft, powdery sands beneath you. The sensation of warm sand between your toes, coupled with the mesmerizing vistas stretching out before you, creates a sensory experience that is both soothing and invigorating. Breathe in the fresh, salty air, tinged with the scents of the sea and nearby vegetation, as you revel in the natural beauty that surrounds you.

Capo Rizzuto offers the perfect opportunity for a leisurely swim in its tranquil waters. The calm and clear Ionian Sea beckons you to immerse yourself in its refreshing embrace, providing a sense of rejuvenation and revitalization. Whether you choose to wade in the shallows, feeling the gentle caress of the waves against your skin, or venture further into the sea for a leisurely swim, the pristine waters of Capo Rizzuto offer a serene oasis for aquatic relaxation.

For those seeking the ultimate in relaxation, Capo Rizzuto provides ample space for sunbathing. Find a comfortable spot on the beach, spread out your towel or lounge chair, and let the golden rays of the sun warm your skin. Close your eyes and listen to the soothing sounds of the sea, as you surrender to a state of pure bliss. As time seems to slow down, you'll find yourself completely absorbed in the peaceful surroundings, leaving behind the worries and stresses of everyday life.

The beauty of Capo Rizzuto lies not only in its picturesque beaches but also in its untouched landscapes. Take a moment to appreciate the breathtaking views that stretch out before you. Marvel at the shimmering expanse of the sea, its hues of blue and green merging seamlessly with the horizon. Scan the coastline, dotted with coves, cliffs, and natural rock formations, creating a stunning backdrop against the azure waters. It's a sight that will leave an indelible impression on your heart and mind.

Capo Rizzuto's allure lies in its ability to transport you to a world of pure tranquility and natural beauty. It invites you to unwind, disconnect from the outside world, and immerse yourself in the blissful ambiance of the Ionian Coastline. Whether you choose to take leisurely walks, enjoy a refreshing swim, or simply bask in the warmth of the sun, Capo Rizzuto promises an unforgettable experience that will rejuvenate your senses and leave you with cherished memories of Calabria's coastal paradise.

The charm of Capo Rizzuto extends beyond its natural beauty. The area is also known for its rich biodiversity and vibrant marine life, making it a haven for nature enthusiasts and snorkeling enthusiasts alike. As you venture into the crystal-clear waters, you'll have the opportunity to witness the vibrant underwater world that thrives beneath the surface. Explore the colorful coral reefs and swim alongside schools of fish, immersing yourself in an aquatic spectacle that will leave you in awe.

For those seeking a more active adventure, Capo Rizzuto offers a variety of water sports and activities to satisfy your adventurous spirit. Dive into the waves with a thrilling session of surfing or paddleboarding, harnessing the power of the sea as you ride the rolling swells. Embark on a kayaking expedition, gliding through the calm waters, and exploring hidden coves and inlets that can only be accessed from the sea. The options are endless, ensuring that there's something for everyone to enjoy along the vibrant coast of Capo Rizzuto.

If you find yourself in need of a break from the beach, Capo Rizzuto's surrounding landscape beckons you to explore its natural wonders. Lace up your hiking boots and venture into the nearby nature reserves, where you'll discover lush forests, scenic trails, and breathtaking viewpoints. Immerse yourself in the tranquility of the Mediterranean scrubland, where fragrant herbs and wildflowers perfume the air. Keep an eye out for native wildlife, from colorful butterflies to elusive bird species, as you wander through this pristine natural environment.

When it comes to culinary delights, Capo Rizzuto doesn't disappoint. Indulge in the flavors of Calabria by sampling fresh seafood dishes that showcase the region's coastal bounty. From succulent grilled fish to seafood pasta delicacies, each bite is a celebration of the local gastronomy. Savor the fusion of traditional recipes and Mediterranean influences, accompanied by a glass of local wine or the refreshing citrus-infused limoncello.

As the sun begins to set, casting a golden glow over the landscape, the magic of Capo Rizzuto becomes even more apparent. Find a cozy spot along the shoreline to witness nature's own masterpiece—the captivating sunset over the Ionian Sea. The sky transforms into a canvas of vibrant hues, painting strokes of orange, pink, and purple, creating a breathtaking spectacle that will forever be etched in your memory.

Capo Rizzuto is a coastal paradise that invites you to slow down, reconnect with nature, and embrace the simple pleasures of life. Whether you seek relaxation, adventure, or a taste of local culture, this coastal gem on the Ionian Coastline of Calabria has it all. So, allow yourself to be captivated by the tranquility, beauty, and charm of Capo Rizzuto as you create memories that will last a lifetime.

Riace Marina:
Riace Marina, a coastal town along the Ionian Coastline of Calabria, is truly a hidden gem renowned for its captivating beauty and pristine beaches. As you approach Riace Marina, you'll be greeted by a breathtaking sight—the crystalline waters of the Ionian Sea, reflecting shades of turquoise and emerald. The vibrant hues of the sea create an enchanting backdrop that invites you to immerse yourself in its splendor.

The unspoiled beaches of Riace Marina offer a tranquil and peaceful setting, allowing you to escape from the hustle and bustle of daily life. Feel the soft, warm sand beneath your feet as you find your perfect spot to relax and unwind. The rhythmic sound of the waves gently lapping against the shore creates a soothing melody that lulls you into a state of pure bliss. You can stretch out on a beach towel, bask in the sun's gentle warmth, and indulge in the simple pleasure of watching the sea's ebb and flow.

For those seeking adventure, Riace Marina presents ample opportunities for water activities. Grab your snorkeling gear and explore the vibrant underwater world that lies just beneath the surface. The clear visibility of the water allows you to witness the mesmerizing marine life and discover the colorful coral reefs that thrive in these pristine coastal waters. Dive deeper with a scuba diving excursion and uncover hidden treasures that lay hidden beneath the waves.

Riace Marina's coastal landscape is teeming with natural wonders. Venture beyond the beach and explore the surrounding cliffs and coves, which offer picturesque views and secluded spots for peaceful contemplation. Embark on a leisurely coastal walk, allowing the sea breeze to invigorate your senses and the panoramic vistas to take your breath away.

When it comes to culinary delights, Riace Marina doesn't disappoint. Indulge in the freshest seafood caught from the nearby waters, prepared with traditional Calabrian flavors that will tantalize your taste buds. Local restaurants and seaside cafes offer a delightful array of dishes that showcase the region's culinary heritage, allowing you to savor the flavors of the sea while enjoying the coastal ambiance.

Riace Marina embodies the essence of coastal serenity and natural beauty, offering a sanctuary where you can reconnect with nature and rejuvenate your soul. Whether you choose to simply relax on the beach, embark on underwater adventures, or explore the stunning coastal landscapes, Riace Marina will leave an indelible mark on your heart and soul. It's a place where the vibrant colors of the sea merge with the tranquility of the surroundings, creating a truly mesmerizing experience that will stay with you long after you've left its shores.

The allure of Riace Marina extends beyond its picturesque beaches and vibrant waters. The town itself is a charming coastal retreat, exuding a laid-back atmosphere that immediately puts you at ease. As you wander through its streets, you'll encounter quaint shops, local boutiques, and inviting cafes where you can indulge in a leisurely cup of coffee or sample traditional Calabrian delicacies.

In addition to its natural beauty, Riace Marina is known for its warm hospitality and friendly locals. The town embraces visitors with open arms, eager to share their love for this coastal paradise. Strike up a conversation with the residents, and you'll discover a genuine warmth and a deep-rooted pride in their beloved Riace Marina.

To fully immerse yourself in the wonders of Riace Marina, take advantage of the various water activities available. Snorkeling enthusiasts will be treated to an underwater spectacle, encountering colorful fish, delicate sea anemones, and even the occasional sighting of marine turtles. The clear, transparent waters allow for a truly immersive experience, where you can explore the hidden treasures of the sea firsthand.

For those seeking a more exhilarating adventure, scuba diving in Riace Marina is an absolute must. Dive deeper into the depths of the Ionian Sea, discovering ancient shipwrecks, underwater caves, and awe-inspiring rock formations. The experienced dive centers in the area cater to divers of all levels, ensuring a safe and unforgettable exploration of the marine wonders that lie beneath the surface.

As the day winds down, the sunset over Riace Marina paints a picture-perfect scene. Find a quiet spot along the shoreline, and witness the sky ablaze with hues of orange, pink, and gold as the sun slowly descends into the horizon. The tranquil ambiance of this coastal haven is further heightened during these magical moments, providing an opportunity for reflection and gratitude.

Riace Marina is not just a destination; it's an experience that lingers in your memories long after you depart. Its captivating beauty, pristine beaches, and warm hospitality combine to create an enchanting coastal marvel that captures the hearts of all who visit. Whether you seek relaxation, adventure, or a cultural immersion, Riace Marina offers a slice of paradise on the Ionian Coastline, leaving you with an indelible connection to this idyllic coastal town.

Soverato:
Soverato, often hailed as the "Pearl of the Ionian Sea," is a vibrant coastal town that perfectly embodies the essence of a Mediterranean beach destination. Nestled along the stunning Ionian Coastline of Calabria, Soverato offers an enchanting blend of natural beauty, modern amenities, and a lively atmosphere that captivates visitors.

The main draw of Soverato is undoubtedly its pristine beach, which stretches along the azure waters, creating a picturesque setting that is hard to resist. As you set foot on the soft sands, you'll be greeted by a sight that epitomizes paradise. The beach is lined with swaying palm trees, providing natural shade and a tropical ambiance. The crystal-clear waters invite you to take a refreshing dip, while the gentle waves beckon for a swim or some exciting water sports adventures.

For sunseekers and beach enthusiasts, Soverato offers the perfect playground. Whether you choose to bask under the warm sun, lounge on a beach chair, or spread out a towel on the sand, you'll find your own little slice of paradise. The beach clubs scattered along the shoreline provide additional comfort and convenience, offering amenities such as umbrellas, sun loungers, and beachside services. You can indulge in a day of sunbathing, swimming, and building sandcastles with your loved ones.

Soverato's charm extends beyond its beach. The town boasts a charming promenade that buzzes with activity. As you stroll along the promenade, you'll be captivated by the vibrant atmosphere and the array of restaurants, cafes, and shops that line the street. Here, you can tantalize your taste buds with local delicacies, savoring the flavors of freshly caught seafood, traditional Calabrian dishes, and gelato. The cafes offer a perfect spot for people-watching and enjoying a leisurely cup of coffee, while the shops showcase local crafts, souvenirs, and fashion.

The evenings in Soverato come alive with a vibrant nightlife scene. The town offers a diverse range of entertainment options, including live music performances, beach parties, and bustling bars where you can dance the night away. Soverato's lively nightlife attracts both locals and tourists, creating an energetic and festive atmosphere that adds an extra layer of excitement to your stay.

Beyond the beach and promenade, Soverato serves as a gateway to further exploration. From here, you can embark on boat tours, exploring the nearby islands and hidden coves. You can also venture into the surrounding countryside to discover charming villages, vineyards, and olive groves, immersing yourself in the authentic Calabrian lifestyle.

In Soverato, you'll find the perfect blend of natural beauty, modern amenities, and a lively coastal atmosphere. It is a place where you can unwind, indulge in the pleasures of the beach, savor delicious cuisine, and immerse yourself in the vibrant local culture. Whether you're seeking relaxation, adventure, or a taste of the Mediterranean lifestyle, Soverato delivers an unforgettable experience that will leave you with cherished memories of your time on the Ionian Coastline.

Soverato, the "Pearl of the Ionian Sea," offers a plethora of activities and attractions that go beyond its stunning beach and lively promenade. The town is a gateway to experiencing the rich cultural heritage and natural wonders of the region.

For history enthusiasts, a visit to the nearby ancient Greek ruins of Locri Epizephiri is a must. Just a short drive from Soverato, this archaeological site allows you to step back in time and explore the remnants of an ancient city. Wander through the ancient streets, marvel at the well-preserved mosaics, and discover the fascinating history of this once-thriving civilization.

Nature lovers will find solace in the nearby natural parks and reserves that showcase the diverse landscapes of Calabria. The Sila National Park, with its lush forests, majestic mountains, and serene lakes, offers opportunities for hiking, biking, and immersing yourself in the beauty of nature. The Aspromonte National Park, characterized by its rugged terrain and rich biodiversity, is home to rare wildlife species and offers breathtaking hiking trails for all levels of outdoor enthusiasts.

For those seeking a taste of authentic Calabrian cuisine, Soverato and its surrounding areas are a culinary paradise. Indulge in the region's renowned seafood dishes, such as fresh swordfish, prawns, and anchovies. Sample traditional specialties like 'nduja, a spicy spreadable salami, or dig into a plate of handmade pasta served with flavorful Calabrian sauces. Don't forget to pair your meal with a glass of local wine, as Calabria is known for its vineyards and rich winemaking traditions.

Venturing a bit further from Soverato, you can explore the charming coastal towns and hidden gems that dot the Ionian Coastline. Visit the picturesque village of Stilo, known for its Byzantine architecture and the iconic Cattolica di Stilo, a Byzantine-style church perched on a hilltop. Take a day trip to the enchanting town of Gerace, with its medieval atmosphere, winding streets, and panoramic views of the surrounding countryside.

Outdoor enthusiasts will find plenty of water sports and activities to enjoy along the Ionian Coastline. From jet skiing and paddleboarding to sailing and snorkeling, there are endless opportunities to make a splash in the crystal-clear waters. Charter a boat to explore secluded coves and hidden beaches, or embark on a fishing excursion to try your hand at catching your own dinner.

Soverato truly offers something for everyone, whether you're seeking relaxation, adventure, history, or culinary delights. The town's vibrant energy, combined with its natural beauty and proximity to cultural and natural attractions, makes it an ideal base for exploring the wonders of the Ionian Coastline and immersing yourself in the essence of Calabria.

Immerse yourself in the vibrant ambiance, indulge in the local flavors, and create unforgettable memories as you discover the coastal marvels of Soverato and its surrounding areas.

Punta Stilo:
Punta Stilo stands as a testament to the rugged beauty of the Ionian Coastline, captivating visitors with its picturesque landscape and awe-inspiring vistas. This stunning cape offers panoramic views that stretch across the azure sea, providing a breathtaking backdrop that beckons photographers to capture its natural splendor.

One of the highlights of Punta Stilo is its ancient ruins, which offer a fascinating glimpse into Calabria's rich historical heritage. Among these ruins is a Greek temple, standing as a reminder of the region's ancient past. Immerse yourself in history as you explore the remnants of this ancient sanctuary, marveling at the architectural marvels and contemplating the stories they hold.

Perched atop the cape is a Byzantine watchtower, a vestige of the region's medieval history. This watchtower once served as a strategic lookout point, offering protection and surveillance over the surrounding coastline. Today, it stands as a symbol of resilience and a testament to the region's cultural heritage. Climb its sturdy steps and reach the top, where panoramic views of the Ionian Sea await, allowing you to appreciate the cape's natural beauty from a different perspective.

While exploring Punta Stilo, take a leisurely stroll along the cliffside paths that wind their way through the rugged terrain. As you walk, relish in the stunning vistas that unfold before you, with the sparkling sea stretching as far as the eye can see. The combination of dramatic cliffs, lush vegetation, and the ever-present sound of crashing waves creates a sensory experience that is both invigorating and serene.

Allow yourself to be captivated by the captivating natural surroundings that Punta Stilo offers. The salty sea breeze caresses your face, and the scent of wildflowers mingles with the ocean air. Take a moment to sit on a sun-warmed rock, listening to the rhythmic sounds of the waves crashing against the cliffs. As you gaze out into the horizon, you may even catch a glimpse of passing sailboats or playful dolphins dancing in the distance.

Punta Stilo is not just a destination; it's an invitation to connect with nature, history, and the spirit of Calabria. It's a place where the past intertwines with the present, where the beauty of the landscape harmonizes with the echoes of ancient civilizations. Whether you're an avid photographer, a history enthusiast, or a nature lover, Punta Stilo offers a captivating experience that will leave an indelible mark on your journey along the Ionian Coastline.

As you continue your exploration of Punta Stilo, you'll discover that its beauty extends beyond its panoramic views and ancient ruins. The cape's rugged coastline is adorned with an abundance of natural wonders that further enhance its allure.

Follow the cliffside paths that meander along Punta Stilo, and you'll be rewarded with glimpses of hidden coves and secluded beaches nestled between the cliffs. These pristine stretches of sand offer a peaceful retreat where you can relax, sunbathe, or take a refreshing swim in the clear, turquoise waters. The secluded nature of these beaches adds to their charm, providing a sense of tranquility and seclusion that allows you to fully immerse yourself in the coastal paradise.

As you traverse the paths, keep an eye out for the unique flora and fauna that call Punta Stilo home. The rugged terrain supports a variety of plant species, from resilient shrubs to colorful wildflowers that blanket the landscape with bursts of vibrant hues. If you're lucky, you may even spot some native wildlife, such as birds soaring overhead or small marine creatures along the water's edge.

For the more adventurous souls, Punta Stilo offers opportunities for exploration and outdoor activities. Embark on a kayaking adventure along the coastline, gliding through the calm waters and marveling at the towering cliffs from a different perspective. Alternatively, venture into the crystal-clear sea for a snorkeling or diving excursion, where you can discover the underwater world teeming with marine life and vibrant coral formations.

As the day draws to a close, find a serene spot along Punta Stilo to witness the breathtaking sunset. The sky transforms into a vibrant canvas, ablaze with hues of orange, pink, and purple, casting a golden glow over the cape and the glistening sea. It's a moment of pure tranquility and natural beauty that will leave an indelible imprint on your heart.

Punta Stilo is a destination that invites you to slow down, embrace the beauty of nature, and connect with the rich history that permeates the region. It's a place where the rugged coastal landscape merges seamlessly with ancient ruins, creating a tapestry of captivating sights and experiences. Whether you choose to immerse yourself in the history, bask in the natural splendor, or simply find solace in the serenity of the surroundings, Punta Stilo will leave you with memories that linger long after you've bid farewell to its shores.

Le Castella:

Le Castella, nestled along the Ionian Coastline, is a small seaside village that captivates visitors with its enchanting blend of history, beauty, and coastal charm. The village is renowned for its most prominent landmark, the remarkable Aragonese castle. This medieval fortress, perched on a rocky peninsula that juts into the sea, stands as a testament to the region's rich historical heritage.

As you approach Le Castella, your eyes will be drawn to the imposing walls and watchtowers of the Aragonese castle, which date back to the 16th century. This architectural masterpiece served as a strategic stronghold against invasions and pirate attacks, offering a glimpse into the region's turbulent past. Walking through the castle's gates, you'll step into a world frozen in time, where centuries of history come alive.

Explore the castle's interior, wandering through its well-preserved rooms and courtyards. Marvel at the intricate details of the architecture and imagine the lives of the knights and nobles who once resided within its walls. From the castle's elevated vantage point, you'll be treated to panoramic views of the Ionian Sea, offering a breathtaking backdrop to the village and surrounding coastline.

Leaving the castle, venture into the village itself, where charming streets beckon you to explore further. Lined with cozy cafes, inviting restaurants, and artisanal souvenir shops, the village invites you to immerse yourself in its laid-back atmosphere. Take leisurely strolls along the narrow streets, taking in the colorful facades and quaint squares adorned with blooming flowers.

The shoreline of Le Castella is a true gem, with its pristine beaches and crystal-clear waters. As you walk along the coast, the invigorating sea breeze gently brushes against your skin, heightening your senses. Find a secluded spot to relax on the golden sands, listen to the rhythmic sounds of the waves crashing against the shore, and feel a sense of serenity wash over you.

Le Castella is also renowned for its delectable seafood cuisine, which is a must-try during your visit. Indulge in fresh catches of the day at the local restaurants, savoring the flavors of the sea that have been perfected by generations of fishermen and chefs. From succulent grilled fish to mouthwatering seafood pasta dishes, the culinary offerings of Le Castella will tantalize your taste buds.

Le Castella's allure extends beyond its castle and coastal beauty. The village boasts a warm and welcoming atmosphere, with locals eager to share their stories and traditions. As you engage with the friendly residents, you'll gain insights into the authentic Calabrian way of life and the village's deep-rooted cultural heritage.

Immerse yourself in Le Castella's cultural offerings by visiting the local museums and art galleries. These venues showcase the region's artistic talents, historical artifacts, and folkloric traditions. Admire vibrant paintings depicting the local landscapes, learn about the village's historical significance through fascinating exhibits, and discover the rich tapestry of Calabrian culture that has shaped Le Castella.

For those seeking adventure, Le Castella offers opportunities for exploration both on land and at sea. Embark on a scenic hike along the rugged coastline, following paths that lead to hidden coves and panoramic viewpoints. The pristine waters invite you to discover the underwater wonders through snorkeling or diving excursions, where you can witness the vibrant marine life thriving beneath the surface.

Le Castella is also a gateway to discovering the natural splendors of the surrounding area. Take a boat trip to nearby marine reserves, where you can marvel at the diverse marine ecosystems and swim in crystal-clear waters teeming with colorful fish. Alternatively, venture inland to explore the picturesque countryside, dotted with olive groves, vineyards, and charming rural villages.

Throughout the year, Le Castella hosts lively festivals and events that celebrate the village's cultural heritage. From traditional music performances to gastronomic feasts showcasing local specialties, these festivities offer a glimpse into the vibrant traditions and communal spirit that define Calabria. Join in the festivities, dance to traditional folk tunes, and savor the flavors of authentic Calabrian cuisine.

As the sun begins to set, the village takes on a magical glow, and the waterfront promenade comes alive with a lively ambiance. Join locals and fellow travelers at seaside bars and restaurants, enjoying a leisurely evening stroll along the water's edge. Indulge in a romantic dinner as you watch the sun dip below the horizon, casting hues of orange and pink across the sky.

Le Castella is a place where history intertwines with natural beauty, creating an unforgettable experience for all who visit. Whether you're a history enthusiast, a nature lover, or a seeker of cultural immersion, this small seaside village along the Ionian Coastline will captivate you with its unique blend of heritage, charm, and coastal allure.

Roccella Ionica:
Roccella Ionica, nestled along the Ionian Coastline of Calabria, is a coastal town that seamlessly blends history, culture, and natural beauty. Its charming historic center

transports you back in time with its narrow streets, ancient churches, and picturesque squares.

As you enter the old quarter of Roccella Ionica, you'll feel as if you've stepped into a living postcard. The narrow, winding streets are lined with centuries-old buildings, exuding an aura of timeless beauty. Explore at a leisurely pace, allowing yourself to get lost among the hidden corners and alleyways that hold stories of the past. Admire the architectural treasures that grace the historic center, from ornate facades to intricately designed doorways.

The ancient churches of Roccella Ionica stand as testaments to the town's religious and cultural heritage. Step inside these sacred spaces to marvel at the breathtaking frescoes, elaborate altars, and hushed atmosphere. The echoes of history can be felt within the walls of these holy sites, offering a glimpse into the spiritual and artistic traditions of the region.

Beyond its historical charm, Roccella Ionica is blessed with beautiful beaches that beckon visitors to unwind and embrace the coastal serenity. The town's golden sands stretch along the shoreline, inviting you to spread out a beach towel and bask in the warmth of the sun. The clear waters of the Ionian Sea entice you to take refreshing dips, providing respite from the summer heat. Whether you prefer to relax under a beach umbrella with a good book, build sandcastles with your family, or partake in water sports activities such as snorkeling or paddleboarding, Roccella Ionica's beaches offer a variety of options to suit your preferences.

The town's blend of history and natural beauty creates a captivating atmosphere that draws visitors from near and far. The juxtaposition of the ancient and the coastal provides a unique experience, where you can immerse yourself in the richness of Roccella Ionica's cultural heritage while also enjoying the tranquility and splendor of its beaches.

In the evenings, the town comes alive with a vibrant energy as locals and visitors gather in the squares and waterfront promenade. Indulge in the local cuisine at the charming restaurants and trattorias, savoring fresh seafood and traditional Calabrian dishes. As the sun sets over the Ionian Sea, casting a warm glow on the town, the enchantment of Roccella Ionica deepens, leaving you with a sense of wonder and a desire to return.

Beyond its historical charm and beautiful beaches, Roccella Ionica offers a myriad of experiences that further enhance its allure. Immerse yourself in the town's cultural scene by attending one of its lively festivals or events. From traditional music performances to art exhibitions, Roccella Ionica showcases its artistic heritage and vibrant community spirit.

For those seeking adventure, the surrounding natural landscapes provide ample opportunities for exploration. Take a hike along the scenic trails that wind through the hills and forests surrounding Roccella Ionica, offering breathtaking panoramic views of the coastline. Discover hidden coves and secluded beaches accessible only by foot, rewarding you with a sense of discovery and tranquility.

History enthusiasts can delve deeper into the town's past by visiting its museums and archaeological sites. The Museo Archeologico di Roccella Ionica houses a collection of artifacts that unveil the region's ancient history, including Greek and Roman artifacts. Explore the ruins of ancient settlements such as Locri Epizephiri and Kaulon, where you can walk amidst the remnants of temples, amphitheaters, and ancient city walls, transporting yourself back to the time of ancient civilizations.

Roccella Ionica's culinary scene is also a delight for food lovers. Sample the flavors of Calabria by indulging in traditional dishes and local specialties. From freshly caught seafood to robust pasta dishes and artisanal cheeses, the town's restaurants and trattorias offer a gastronomic journey through the region's culinary traditions. Don't forget to pair your meal with a glass of local wine or limoncello, made from the citrus groves that dot the landscape.

As you meander through the streets of Roccella Ionica, you'll encounter friendly locals who are eager to share their stories and traditions. Engage in conversation, learn about their way of life, and perhaps even partake in a cooking class or traditional craft workshop to immerse yourself in the local culture.

Whether you're seeking relaxation, cultural immersion, outdoor adventures, or a culinary exploration, Roccella Ionica has something to offer every visitor. Its blend of history, natural beauty, and warm hospitality create an atmosphere that is both captivating and welcoming. Allow yourself to be enchanted by the charm of Roccella Ionica as you create lasting memories and discover the hidden treasures of this coastal marvel along the Ionian Coastline of Calabria.

Exploring these coastal marvels along the Ionian Coastline will give you a deeper appreciation for the stunning beauty and rich cultural heritage of Calabria. Whether you're seeking relaxation, historical exploration, or simply a picturesque beach getaway, these destinations offer an unforgettable experience that will leave you with lasting memories.

Chapter 3: Historic Treasures of Calabria

Reggio Calabria

Reggio Calabria, the largest city in Calabria, is a treasure trove of historical and cultural wonders. In this chapter, we will explore some of its prominent attractions.

Museo Nazionale della Magna Grecia

The Museo Nazionale della Magna Graecia in Reggio Calabria stands as a treasure trove of historical artifacts, offering an immersive experience for history enthusiasts. This renowned museum is a must-visit destination for those eager to delve into the ancient Greek colonies that once thrived in Calabria.

As you step inside the museum, you will be greeted by a vast and diverse collection of artifacts that date back to the period of Magna Graecia, the name given to the Greek settlements in Southern Italy. The museum's exhibits provide a fascinating glimpse into the region's rich ancient past and shed light on the cultural and artistic achievements of the Greek colonists.

One of the highlights of the museum is its extraordinary collection of statues. Marvel at the exquisite craftsmanship and lifelike representations of the human form. From graceful sculptures of Greek gods and goddesses to powerful depictions of mythological figures, each statue tells a story and evokes a sense of awe.

The museum's display of intricate pottery is equally captivating. Admire the finely painted vases, bowls, and other ceramic vessels that showcase the exceptional skill and artistic expression of the ancient craftsmen. These artifacts provide insights into daily life, religious practices, and artistic traditions of the ancient Greeks.

As you wander through the museum, you will also encounter a wide range of archaeological finds. Explore the preserved remnants of ancient architecture, such as fragments of temples, columns, and architectural decorations. These remnants offer a tangible connection to the past and allow you to envision the grandeur of the Greek colonies that once flourished in Calabria.

The Museo Nazionale della Magna Graecia provides a comprehensive overview of the historical and cultural significance of the ancient Greek settlements in Calabria. It offers a unique opportunity to explore the roots of Western civilization and gain a deeper appreciation for the enduring impact of the ancient Greeks.

Within the Museo Nazionale della Magna Graecia, each artifact tells a story of the cultural, religious, and artistic practices that shaped the lives of the ancient Greeks in Calabria. The museum's curators have meticulously organized the exhibits, allowing visitors to follow a chronological and thematic journey through time.

As you explore the displays, you will encounter a wide array of archaeological finds, including everyday objects that offer glimpses into the daily lives of the ancient inhabitants. Delicate jewelry, intricately designed pottery, and tools used in various trades showcase the craftsmanship and ingenuity of the ancient Greeks. These artifacts not only provide insight into their practical aspects but also offer clues about their aesthetic sensibilities and societal norms.

The museum's collection of statues is particularly breathtaking. Carved from various types of marble and stone, these sculptures showcase the incredible talent of Greek artists. From the serene and idealized depictions of deities to the realistic and emotive representations of human figures, the statues reflect the Greeks' appreciation for beauty, harmony, and the human form.

As you move through the museum, you may also encounter artifacts that highlight the religious practices and beliefs of the ancient Greeks. From votive offerings and sacred objects to depictions of mythological scenes, these pieces provide a glimpse into the spiritual world of the ancient Greeks and their reverence for their gods and goddesses.

The Museo Nazionale della Magna Graecia not only presents individual artifacts but also contextualizes them within the broader historical and cultural framework of Magna Graecia. Descriptive panels and informative displays offer valuable background information, shedding light on the historical significance of each object and its relevance to the region.

For those interested in diving deeper into the fascinating world of Magna Graecia, the museum also hosts temporary exhibitions and educational programs. These events delve into specific themes or showcase new discoveries, providing visitors with fresh insights into the ancient Greek colonies and their enduring legacy.

A visit to the Museo Nazionale della Magna Graecia is a journey back in time, allowing you to appreciate the rich heritage of Calabria and its deep connections to ancient Greek civilization. Prepare to be captivated by the artistry, craftsmanship, and historical significance of the artifacts on display as you uncover the secrets of Magna Graecia and the remarkable contributions of the ancient Greeks to the region.

Promenade of Falcomatà

Stroll along the Promenade of Falcomatà, and allow yourself to be immersed in the enchanting beauty of this remarkable waterfront promenade. Stretching along the coast of Reggio Calabria, the Promenade of Falcomatà offers an unforgettable experience for visitors.

As you embark on your leisurely walk, prepare to be captivated by the awe-inspiring views of the Ionian Sea that unfold before you. The promenade provides unobstructed vistas of the sparkling azure waters, where the sea meets the sky in a seamless horizon. The sight is truly breathtaking, inviting you to pause and marvel at the natural wonders that surround you.

Lined with elegant palm trees, the promenade exudes a sense of sophistication and tranquility. These towering trees provide shade and lend an exotic touch to the landscape, creating a picturesque backdrop against the backdrop of the sea. The swaying of their fronds in the gentle sea breeze adds a soothing soundtrack to your stroll, enhancing the sensory experience.

As you continue along the promenade, take the time to appreciate the meticulously maintained flowerbeds that adorn the pathway. Bursting with vibrant colors, these floral displays create a delightful feast for the eyes. The scents of the blooming flowers perfume the air, enveloping you in their sweet fragrance and heightening the sensory delight.

Along the way, you will encounter charming cafes and inviting restaurants that dot the promenade. Pause for a moment to indulge in a cup of freshly brewed coffee or savor a delectable meal while basking in the serene Mediterranean ambiance. The waterfront setting provides a tranquil and idyllic atmosphere, making it the perfect spot to relax and unwind.

Whether you choose to visit during the daytime or embark on an evening stroll, the Promenade of Falcomatà offers an ever-changing landscape. The shifting colors of the sky, the gentle ebb and flow of the tides, and the play of sunlight on the water create a mesmerizing tableau. It is a place where time seems to stand still, allowing you to fully immerse yourself in the beauty of nature.

Allow yourself to be transported to a world of serenity and relaxation as you continue your stroll along the Promenade of Falcomatà. As you walk, you'll notice that the promenade is not just a visual delight but also offers a range of engaging experiences.

Find a comfortable bench or a spot on the promenade's well-manicured lawns and immerse yourself in the sounds of nature. The rhythmic lapping of the waves against the shore creates a soothing symphony, providing a peaceful soundtrack to your leisurely walk. Close your eyes for a moment and let the melody of the sea wash over you, relieving any stress or worries you may have brought with you.

In addition to its natural allure, the promenade is adorned with artistic elements that add a touch of elegance to the surroundings. Along the pathway, you'll come across captivating sculptures and art installations that celebrate the creativity and cultural heritage of the region. These artistic treasures serve as focal points, inviting contemplation and sparking conversations among visitors.

As you meander along the promenade, keep an eye out for street performers who contribute to the vibrant atmosphere. Talented musicians, artists, and entertainers showcase their skills, enhancing the overall ambiance with their captivating performances. Take a moment to appreciate their talents and perhaps even join in the lively atmosphere by supporting local artists and artisans.

The Promenade of Falcomatà is not just a place for leisurely strolls; it also offers opportunities for active pursuits. Lace up your walking or running shoes and take advantage of the pathway's length to engage in a refreshing jog or invigorating exercise. The invigorating sea breeze and the breathtaking scenery make it an ideal setting for outdoor activities.

As you reach the end of your journey along the promenade, turn around and take one last look at the panoramic views that have accompanied you throughout your walk. Let the memory of the expansive Ionian Sea, the palm trees, and the vibrant flowerbeds leave an indelible imprint on your mind and heart.

The Promenade of Falcomatà is a testament to the beauty of Reggio Calabria and its connection to the sea. It invites you to slow down, immerse yourself in the natural wonders around you, and savor every moment of your visit. Whether you're seeking tranquility, inspiration, or simply a peaceful escape, this elegant esplanade offers a sanctuary for all those who venture along its captivating path.

Chiesa degli Ottimati

Chiesa degli Ottimati, also known as the Church of the Ottimati, stands as a remarkable religious site in the heart of

Reggio Calabria. This historic church, dating back to the 17th century, showcases an impressive example of Baroque architecture that captivates visitors with its grandeur and intricate details.

As you approach the church, you'll be greeted by an exquisite façade adorned with ornate stonework and decorative elements. The façade's design reflects the Baroque style prevalent during the time of its construction, featuring elaborate sculptures, columns, and intricate reliefs that tell stories from religious history.

Upon entering the church, you'll be immersed in a world of beauty and tranquility. The interior of Chiesa degli Ottimati is a testament to the devotion and artistic prowess of its creators. Intricately carved wooden altars, adorned with gold leaf accents, serve as focal points within the space. These altars house religious icons and statues that hold deep spiritual significance for the local community.

As you walk through the church, your eyes will be drawn to the stunning frescoes adorning the walls and ceilings. These masterpieces of religious art depict scenes from biblical narratives, saints, and martyrs, created with meticulous attention to detail and vibrant colors that have withstood the test of time.

The atmosphere within Chiesa degli Ottimati is serene and contemplative, inviting visitors to reflect upon the region's religious heritage. The soft glow of candlelight illuminates the space, adding to the church's ethereal ambiance. The scent of incense wafts through the air, creating a sensory experience that heightens the spiritual connection.

In addition to its architectural and artistic beauty, Chiesa degli Ottimati serves as an important gathering place for the local community. It hosts religious ceremonies, weddings, and other significant events that bring people together in celebration of their faith.

The Chiesa degli Ottimati holds a special place in the hearts of the local community in Reggio Calabria. It serves as not only a place of worship but also a symbol of their religious and cultural heritage. The church's name, "Ottimati," refers to the noble families who were influential in the region during the 17th century.

Inside the church, you'll be surrounded by a sense of reverence and awe. The soft lighting casts a warm glow upon the ornate decorations, creating a serene and introspective atmosphere. The play of light and shadow enhances the intricate details of the Baroque architectural elements, such as the delicate carvings, elaborate moldings, and gracefully curved arches.

The high altar, the centerpiece of the church, is a sight to behold. Adorned with gilded details and adorned with religious symbols, it commands attention and reverence. The altar is flanked by smaller side altars, each dedicated to different saints or religious themes. These altars feature intricately carved statues and delicate bas-reliefs that depict scenes from religious narratives.

As you explore further, you'll notice the walls adorned with frescoes depicting biblical stories and significant religious figures. These vibrant frescoes, painted by skilled artists of the time, bring to life the stories of faith and provide a visual narrative that enhances the spiritual experience within the church.

The Chiesa degli Ottimati serves as a testament to the devotion and artistic talent of the craftsmen and artists of the past. Their skillful hands have left behind a legacy of beauty and inspiration for generations to come. Every brushstroke, every chisel mark, and every detail within the church's interior reflects their dedication to creating a sacred space that evokes a sense of reverence and spiritual connection.

Visiting the Chiesa degli Ottimati offers a unique opportunity to immerse yourself in the history and spirituality of Reggio Calabria. It provides a glimpse into the region's religious traditions and the artistic legacy that has shaped its cultural identity. Whether you are a religious pilgrim seeking solace or an art enthusiast marveling at the craftsmanship, this remarkable church invites you to experience the profound beauty and serenity that define its essence.

Tropea

Tropea, a charming coastal town located on the Tyrrhenian Coast, is renowned for its rich historical and cultural heritage. In this chapter, we will explore the fascinating historic treasures that Tropea has to offer.

Tropea Cathedral:

Tropea Cathedral, also referred to as the Santa Maria Assunta Cathedral, is an awe-inspiring architectural masterpiece that stands proudly as a dominant feature of Tropea's skyline. This magnificent cathedral is a testament to the enduring beauty of Norman architecture and holds a significant place in the town's history.

Dating back to the 12th century, Tropea Cathedral showcases a harmonious blend of influences from different periods. Its construction began during the Norman era, and subsequent additions and renovations over the centuries have contributed to its unique architectural character.

As visitors approach the cathedral, they are greeted by an extraordinary facade adorned with intricate stone carvings. The facade is a work of art in itself, showcasing exquisite craftsmanship and detailing. Every nook and cranny of the facade tells a story, depicting biblical scenes, saints, and other symbolic representations.

Stepping through the grand entrance, visitors are welcomed into the sanctuary of Tropea Cathedral. The interior is a treasure trove of artistic marvels. The cathedral's nave is adorned with elegant columns, arches, and vaulted ceilings, showcasing the remarkable craftsmanship of the period. The play of light and shadow creates a serene ambiance that invites contemplation and reflection.

One of the focal points of the interior is the elaborately decorated altar. Crafted with meticulous attention to detail, the altar features ornate carvings, gilded accents, and intricate patterns. It serves as the centerpiece of religious ceremonies and a visual representation of devotion and reverence.

Throughout the cathedral, visitors can also admire a collection of religious artwork. From delicate frescoes adorning the walls to intricately crafted statues and religious relics, each piece tells a story and adds to the overall spiritual and artistic experience.

Tropea Cathedral has been a place of worship and pilgrimage for centuries, attracting visitors from near and far. Its sacred atmosphere, architectural splendor, and historical significance make it a must-visit destination for anyone exploring Tropea and seeking a deeper understanding of the region's cultural heritage.

Inside the cathedral, the air is filled with a sense of reverence and spirituality. Visitors are invited to take a moment to soak in the serene atmosphere and appreciate the centuries of devotion that have unfolded within these sacred walls.

As you explore further, you'll notice the interplay of light streaming through stained glass windows, casting vibrant hues upon the polished stone floors. The colors dance and change with the shifting daylight, creating an ethereal ambiance that adds to the cathedral's mystique.

In addition to its architectural and artistic marvels, Tropea Cathedral also holds great historical significance. Over the centuries, it has witnessed the ebb and flow of Tropea's fortunes, surviving wars, invasions, and natural disasters. It has stood as a symbol of strength, resilience, and faith, serving as a sanctuary for the townspeople during turbulent times.

The cathedral's importance extends beyond its physical structure. It serves as a spiritual hub, hosting religious ceremonies, weddings, and baptisms that connect generations and strengthen the ties of the community. The echoes of prayers and hymns reverberate through the sacred space, creating a sense of unity and shared beliefs.

As you venture deeper into the cathedral, you may come across side chapels dedicated to saints or specific religious figures. These smaller sanctuaries offer intimate spaces for contemplation and personal reflection. Ornate altarpieces and statues grace these chapels, each telling its own story and inviting visitors to connect with their own spirituality.

While the exterior of Tropea Cathedral is a commanding presence in the town's skyline, it is the interior that truly captures the imagination and leaves a lasting impression. The skillful craftsmanship, the breathtaking beauty, and the spiritual energy combine to create an experience that transcends time and touches the depths of the soul.

Visiting Tropea Cathedral is not merely a touristic endeavor; it is an opportunity to immerse yourself in the living history of Tropea and to witness the enduring power of faith and artistic expression. Whether you are drawn to its architectural splendor, its religious significance, or simply seeking a moment of tranquility, Tropea Cathedral will leave an indelible mark on your journey through this remarkable town.

Santa Maria dell'Isola:

Perched majestically on a rocky outcrop overlooking the glistening turquoise waters of the Tyrrhenian Sea, Santa Maria dell'Isola stands as a picturesque church that holds a significant place in the history and identity of Tropea. This iconic landmark beckons visitors with its stunning location and remarkable architectural beauty.

To reach Santa Maria dell'Isola, visitors embark on a journey up a scenic staircase carved into the rock, offering a gradual ascent while unveiling breathtaking panoramic views of Tropea's coastline. As you climb higher, the captivating vistas of the crystal-clear sea, the golden beaches, and the charming town below unfold before your eyes. This ascent itself becomes an unforgettable part of the experience, immersing you in the natural beauty that surrounds the church.

Upon reaching the top of the staircase, you are greeted by the sight of the church, which dates back to the 11th century. Its silhouette against the sky is a testament to the enduring devotion and architectural mastery of the past. Step through the entrance and into the tranquil interior, where a sense of serenity envelops you. The subdued lighting and hushed atmosphere create an aura of reverence and contemplation.

Inside Santa Maria dell'Isola, visitors can explore the church's exquisite architectural details, from the gracefully arched windows to the intricate stone carvings that adorn the walls. Marvel at the delicate frescoes that have stood the test of time, each brushstroke telling a story of devotion and artistic mastery. The scent of burning candles mingles with the faint echo of prayers, creating a sacred ambiance that invites introspection.

However, the true allure of Santa Maria dell'Isola extends beyond its sacred walls. Step out onto the church's terrace, and you'll be rewarded with an awe-inspiring panorama. From this elevated vantage point, the expansive views encompass not only the turquoise sea but also the sprawling coastline, stretching as far as the eye can see. The juxtaposition of nature's grandeur and the human touch represented by Tropea's charming architecture creates a harmonious and captivating scene.

Take a moment to absorb the tranquil beauty of Tropea from this vantage point. Watch as the sunlight dances upon the waves, listen to the gentle whispers of the sea breeze, and let the breathtaking scenery captivate your senses. The church's terrace becomes a sanctuary for contemplation, a place where one can reflect upon the timeless connection between nature, spirituality, and human existence.

As you stand on the terrace of Santa Maria dell'Isola, let your gaze sweep across the Tyrrhenian Sea, where the azure waters meet the horizon in a seamless blend of colors. The salty breeze caresses your face, carrying with it a sense of tranquility and a profound connection to the natural world.

It is a moment of pure serenity, where time seems to stand still.

From this elevated position, you can also admire the charming town of Tropea below. The red-tiled roofs of the buildings create a picturesque mosaic against the backdrop of the sea. The narrow streets wind their way through the town, inviting exploration and discovery. The vibrant colors of blooming bougainvillea and cascading flowers add a touch of vibrancy to the scene, infusing it with a sense of life and vitality.

As the sun begins its descent, casting a warm golden glow over the landscape, the atmosphere becomes even more enchanting. The church's terrace becomes a front-row seat to nature's own spectacle—the breathtaking sunset over the Tyrrhenian Sea. The sky transforms into a canvas of vibrant hues, with shades of pink, orange, and purple painting a captivating picture. It is a moment of pure magic, where the beauty of Tropea reaches its crescendo.

As the sun dips below the horizon, casting a blanket of stars across the night sky, Santa Maria dell'Isola takes on a different persona. Illuminated by soft lights, the church stands as a beacon of peace and hope in the darkness. The twinkling lights of the town below add a touch of whimsy to the scene, creating a warm and inviting ambiance.

As you reluctantly leave the terrace and make your way back down the staircase, the memories of Santa Maria dell'Isola stay with you. Its timeless beauty, serene interior, and breathtaking views become a part of your own personal journey. The church's allure lingers in your heart, calling you to return and experience its magic once more.

Santa Maria dell'Isola is not merely a place of worship; it is a sanctuary of the senses. It invites contemplation, appreciation, and a profound connection with the natural world. It is a testament to the intertwined nature of spirituality and the breathtaking beauty of Tropea, leaving an indelible impression on all who have the privilege of visiting.

As you depart from Santa Maria dell'Isola, carry its essence with you—a reminder of the tranquility found in moments of reflection, the power of architectural marvels, and the everlasting beauty of nature. Let the experience of this picturesque church and its panoramic vistas become a cherished memory, forever intertwined with the allure of Tropea and its remarkable history.

Historic Old Town:

Wandering through Tropea's Historic Old Town is a truly captivating experience that transports you back in time. As you venture into its narrow, winding streets, you'll feel a sense of nostalgia and wonder. The Old Town's well-preserved medieval character and charming architecture create an enchanting ambiance that captivates visitors from the moment they step foot in this historical enclave.

The streets of Tropea's Old Town are lined with historic buildings, many of which date back centuries. Each structure has its own unique story to tell, reflecting the rich history and cultural heritage of the region. As you walk along these ancient thoroughfares, you'll find yourself surrounded by architectural gems that showcase the town's illustrious past.

Magnificent palaces with ornate facades and intricate details stand as a testament to Tropea's historical significance. These stately buildings once belonged to noble families and influential figures, and today they serve as reminders of a bygone era. The grandeur of these palaces is truly awe-inspiring, evoking a sense of admiration for the craftsmanship and architectural prowess of the time.

Churches also play a prominent role in Tropea's Historic Old Town. These sacred structures, adorned with beautiful frescoes, elaborate altars, and ornamental details, hold deep cultural and religious significance. They serve as gathering places for the local community and are steeped in centuries of faith and devotion. Whether you step inside to admire the stunning interior or simply marvel at the intricate exteriors, these churches add to the town's timeless allure.

The Old Town is not just a place for architectural marvels; it is also a hub of activity and local life. Charming shops beckon visitors with their unique wares, from handmade crafts to local specialties. As you explore, you'll find yourself tempted to browse through artisanal products, such as handcrafted ceramics, intricate lacework, and traditional textiles. These shops are not just places to shop but also windows into the local culture and craftsmanship.

When it's time to savor the flavors of Tropea, the Old Town won't disappoint. Traditional restaurants, often tucked away in hidden corners, offer a chance to indulge in authentic Calabrian cuisine. From fresh seafood dishes bursting with flavors to hearty pasta dishes featuring locally sourced ingredients, the gastronomic delights of Tropea are a true reflection of the region's culinary heritage. Situated amidst the historical surroundings, these restaurants provide a unique dining experience, where you can immerse yourself in the ambiance while savoring the local flavors.

As you meander through Tropea's Historic Old Town, you'll find yourself captivated by the vibrant atmosphere that permeates its streets. The hustle and bustle of locals going about their daily lives, the scent of freshly brewed coffee wafting from cafes, and the echoes of conversations in the air all contribute to the lively and authentic atmosphere. It's a place where time seems to stand still, allowing you to appreciate the simple pleasures of the past and immerse yourself in the essence of Tropea's history.

In Tropea's Historic Old Town, every corner turned reveals a new discovery, a hidden gem waiting to be uncovered. The combination of its architectural splendors, charming shops, delightful restaurants, and vibrant ambiance creates an irresistible allure that leaves a lasting impression on every visitor fortunate enough to explore this enchanting enclave.
The Historic Old Town of Tropea is not just a static display of history; it's a living, breathing neighborhood that exudes a sense of community and vitality. As you stroll through the winding streets, you'll encounter locals going about their daily routines, exchanging greetings with neighbors, and tending to their businesses. This vibrant atmosphere adds an extra layer of authenticity and charm to the experience of stepping back in time.

The narrow streets of Tropea's Old Town are not only picturesque but also serve as a canvas for local artisans and street performers. Talented craftsmen set up their workshops, displaying their creations and skillfully crafting their unique pieces. You might witness a master potter shaping clay on a wheel or a skilled artist capturing the essence of Tropea's beauty on canvas. These encounters provide an opportunity to appreciate the creativity and artistic traditions that have been passed down through generations.

As you wander further into the Old Town, you'll come across inviting squares and cozy plazas. These open spaces act as meeting points for both locals and visitors, where they can take a moment to relax, people-watch, or strike up a conversation. Cafes spill out onto the cobblestone streets, offering a chance to sit back, sip a freshly brewed espresso, and soak in the atmosphere while admiring the surrounding architectural wonders.

The Historic Old Town is also a treasure trove of hidden alleys and secret passages that beckon you to explore further. You might stumble upon tucked-away courtyards adorned with fragrant flowers, inviting benches where you can pause and appreciate the peaceful surroundings, or charming fountains that provide a refreshing respite from your journey. Each twist and turn reveals new surprises and adds to the sense of adventure as you navigate through this labyrinthine neighborhood.

In the evening, the Old Town undergoes a magical transformation. Soft lighting casts a warm glow on the facades of buildings, creating an enchanting ambiance. The lively hum of conversations and laughter emanates from bustling restaurants and cozy taverns. Candlelit tables are set on outdoor terraces, offering an intimate setting for a romantic dinner or a delightful gathering with friends. The Old Town truly comes alive at night, inviting you to savor the flavors of local cuisine, raise a toast with regional wines, and immerse yourself in the convivial spirit of Tropea.

Whether you're an architecture enthusiast, a history buff, or simply someone who appreciates the timeless beauty of a well-preserved Old Town, Tropea's Historic Quarter offers a journey through the ages. Its narrow streets, historic buildings, bustling squares, and lively atmosphere combine to create an unforgettable experience. As you explore, you'll find yourself enchanted by the palpable sense of history and the seamless blending of past and present in this captivating corner of Tropea.

Cosenza

Cosenza, a vibrant city in Calabria, is a treasure trove of historical and cultural landmarks. Nestled amidst picturesque hills, Cosenza boasts a rich heritage that dates back to ancient times. In this chapter, we explore the iconic Cosenza Cathedral, the renowned Rendano Theatre, and the captivating Open-Air Museum Bilotti (MAB).

Cosenza Cathedral:

Standing majestically in the heart of the city, Cosenza Cathedral, also known as the Cathedral of Santa Maria Assunta, is a true architectural masterpiece that leaves visitors in awe. The cathedral's construction began in the 11th century, and over the centuries, it has witnessed numerous renovations and additions, each contributing to its grandeur. The result is a stunning structure that showcases a harmonious blend of different architectural styles, including Norman, Byzantine, and Gothic influences.

Approaching the cathedral, you'll be struck by its imposing presence, with its soaring towers and intricate facade. The exterior reflects the passage of time, displaying intricate stonework and delicate details that have been meticulously preserved. As you step inside, the true splendor of the cathedral reveals itself.

The interior of Cosenza Cathedral is a sight to behold. Upon entering, you'll be greeted by a breathtaking display of artistry and religious devotion. The walls and ceilings are adorned with intricate frescoes that depict biblical scenes, saints, and heavenly motifs. The vibrant colors and meticulous brushwork transport visitors to a world of spiritual significance and artistic excellence.

Mosaics, another prominent feature of the cathedral's interior, add to its beauty. Delicate tiles meticulously arranged to form intricate patterns and depictions create a mesmerizing visual spectacle. The skill and precision involved in crafting these mosaics are a testament to the artistic talent of the craftsmen of the time.

Throughout the cathedral, ornate decorations embellish every corner, from intricately carved wooden altars to finely crafted metalwork. These details demonstrate the devotion and reverence with which the cathedral was designed and constructed.

The Chapel of St. Gregory stands as a highlight within the cathedral. This sacred space houses precious artworks and relics that hold great significance for the faithful. As you enter the chapel, you'll be surrounded by an atmosphere of tranquility and spiritual devotion. Admire the splendid marble altar, a focal point of the chapel, adorned with delicate carvings and symbolic representations. The beautifully sculpted statues of saints and religious figures that grace the chapel evoke a sense of reverence and devotion.

The cathedral's history is deeply intertwined with the city of Cosenza. Over the centuries, it has played a central role in the religious and cultural life of the community. It has been a witness to important events, celebrations, and gatherings that have shaped the identity of the city and its people.

The Cathedral of Santa Maria Assunta has undergone several renovations and additions throughout its long history. These changes reflect the evolving tastes, architectural styles, and religious practices of different eras. From the original Romanesque design to the incorporation of Gothic elements and the subsequent embellishments in the Renaissance period, each modification contributes to the cathedral's unique character.

As you walk through the cathedral, you'll discover chapels dedicated to various saints and religious figures, each adorned with its own artistic treasures. The craftsmanship and attention to detail in the statues, paintings, and decorations are awe-inspiring. These artworks serve not only as expressions of faith but also as reflections of the cultural and artistic influences of the time.

In addition to its architectural and artistic splendor, Cosenza Cathedral is a place of spiritual significance. It provides a sanctuary for prayer, reflection, and worship. The serene atmosphere inside the cathedral invites visitors to pause, meditate, and connect with their inner selves.

Beyond its religious and artistic significance, the cathedral also serves as a testament to the resilience and perseverance of the people of Cosenza. It has withstood the tests of time, surviving earthquakes, fires, and other challenges. Each restoration and preservation effort has been a testament to the unwavering dedication to preserving this symbol of faith and heritage.

Visiting Cosenza Cathedral allows you to delve into the depths of history, spirituality, and artistic expression. It offers a window into the cultural fabric of the city and provides a tangible connection to its past. Whether you are captivated by its architectural beauty, moved by its religious significance, or simply seeking a moment of tranquility, the cathedral offers a profound and enriching experience that will leave a lasting impression on your journey through Calabria.

Rendano Theatre:

A true cultural gem, the Rendano Theatre stands as an architectural marvel in the city of Cosenza, captivating visitors with its grandeur and rich history. Built in the late 19th century, the theater's exquisite neoclassical façade immediately commands attention as you approach its entrance. The meticulously crafted details and imposing presence evoke a sense of awe, hinting at the artistic wonders that lie within.

Stepping into the theater's grand hall, you are instantly transported to a bygone era of elegance and opulence. The interior of the Rendano Theatre is a testament to the craftsmanship and artistic vision of its creators. Ornate chandeliers cast a soft glow, illuminating the richly decorated walls adorned with intricate frescoes and intricate moldings. Plush velvet seats line the auditorium, providing a luxurious and comfortable setting for the audience.

The Rendano Theatre has established itself as a vibrant hub for performing arts in Cosenza. It proudly hosts a diverse range of performances that cater to various artistic tastes. From grand operas that stir the soul to breathtaking ballets that showcase the grace and skill of dancers, from captivating concerts that fill the air with beautiful melodies to thought-provoking theater productions that ignite the imagination – the theater's programming ensures there is something for everyone to enjoy.

Visiting the Rendano Theatre allows you to immerse yourself in an enchanting atmosphere where the magic of live performances comes to life. As the curtains rise and the performers take the stage, you become captivated by their talent and artistry. The theater's impeccable acoustics enhance the auditory experience, allowing every note of the music and every line of dialogue to resonate with clarity and emotion.

Beyond the artistic performances, the Rendano Theatre itself is a work of art. Its stunning interior design, coupled with the grandeur of the performances, creates a sensory feast for the audience. The combination of visual splendor, masterful performances, and the palpable energy that fills the air makes the Rendano Theatre a must-visit destination for art enthusiasts and culture aficionados alike.

The Rendano Theatre's legacy extends far beyond its architectural splendor and captivating performances. Throughout its history, the theater has played a crucial role in nurturing local talent and fostering a sense of community. It serves as a platform for emerging artists to showcase their skills, providing them with an opportunity to shine on a prestigious stage.

In addition to its regular programming, the Rendano Theatre hosts special events and festivals that celebrate various forms of artistic expression. These events bring together artists, performers, and enthusiasts from near and far, creating a vibrant and dynamic cultural scene within Cosenza. The theater becomes a melting pot of creativity, where different artistic disciplines intersect and inspire one another.

Beyond its impact on the local arts scene, the Rendano Theatre holds a special place in the hearts of the residents of Cosenza. It has become a symbol of pride and identity for the community, representing their appreciation for the performing arts and their commitment to preserving their cultural heritage. The theater serves as a gathering place where people from all walks of life come together to share moments of joy, reflection, and collective experience.

Visiting the Rendano Theatre is not only about witnessing exceptional performances but also about immersing yourself in a cultural phenomenon that has shaped the identity of Cosenza. It allows you to connect with the city's history, its artistic soul, and the passions of its residents. The theater stands as a testament to the enduring power of art to inspire, entertain, and unite people across time and generations.

As you explore Cosenza and delve into its vibrant cultural scene, a visit to the Rendano Theatre is an essential part of your journey. Whether you are a seasoned art lover or simply seeking an unforgettable experience, the theater offers an invitation to be transported to a realm of artistic excellence, where the boundaries of imagination are pushed and the human spirit is uplifted.

The Rendano Theatre is more than just a building; it is a living testament to the beauty and significance of the performing arts. Its neoclassical façade, enchanting interior, and captivating performances combine to create an immersive experience that will leave an indelible mark on your memory. Step inside, be enveloped by the magic, and allow yourself to be swept away by the symphony of emotions that only live performances can evoke.

Open-Air Museum Bilotti (MAB):

Situated in the scenic area of the Old Town, the Open-Air Museum Bilotti (MAB) stands as a testament to Cosenza's dedication to promoting art and cultural heritage. As you step into the museum, you will find yourself immersed in a captivating artistic experience like no other.

MAB offers a unique approach to showcasing contemporary art by placing sculptures and installations throughout the open-air space. The museum seamlessly integrates these modern artworks with the city's historic buildings and narrow streets, creating a dynamic and harmonious visual landscape. The juxtaposition of the contemporary art against the backdrop of Cosenza's rich architectural heritage creates a striking contrast that stimulates the senses and sparks curiosity.

As you stroll through the museum, you will encounter an array of captivating artworks created by renowned artists from Italy and beyond. Each sculpture and installation tells its own story, inviting viewers to interpret and engage with the artwork on a personal level. The artists' use of different materials, forms, and techniques evokes a range of emotions and prompts deep reflection on various themes and concepts.

MAB not only serves as a platform for contemporary artistic expression but also fosters a meaningful dialogue between the past and the present. The juxtaposition of the modern artworks against the ancient surroundings prompts contemplation on the ever-evolving nature of art and its connection to historical context. It serves as a reminder that while the world changes, art continues to be a powerful means of communication and reflection across generations.

Moreover, the Open-Air Museum Bilotti (MAB) serves as a catalyst for artistic appreciation and community engagement. The museum actively encourages interaction between visitors and the artworks, creating an immersive experience that transcends traditional museum boundaries. As you explore the open-air space, you'll find that some sculptures invite tactile exploration or provide interactive elements, inviting you to actively participate in the artistic process.

MAB's collection showcases a diverse range of artistic styles, representing various periods and movements in contemporary art. From abstract sculptures that challenge conventional forms to thought-provoking installations that address social issues, the museum offers a platform for artists to express their creativity and make meaningful statements. By featuring both established and emerging artists, MAB contributes to the ongoing evolution of the art world and supports the development of new talent.

Beyond its artistic significance, the Open-Air Museum Bilotti also plays a vital role in revitalizing the Old Town of Cosenza. The museum's presence attracts visitors from near and far, promoting tourism and stimulating the local economy. As you wander through the narrow streets, you'll discover charming cafes, boutique shops, and local artisans, all benefiting from the increased foot traffic generated by MAB. The museum acts as a cultural hub that breathes new life into the historic district, creating a vibrant and thriving community.

By visiting Cosenza Cathedral, attending a performance at the Rendano Theatre, and exploring the Open-Air Museum Bilotti (MAB), you embark on a holistic journey that encapsulates the essence of Cosenza's cultural and artistic heritage. These iconic landmarks not only offer aesthetic pleasures but also provide opportunities for self-reflection, intellectual stimulation, and connections with the local community. They showcase the city's commitment to preserving its past while embracing the dynamism of the present, making your travel experience in Calabria truly enriching and unforgettable.

Chapter 4: Delving into Calabria's Culinary Delights

In this chapter, we will embark on a gastronomic journey through the flavors and aromas of Calabria. Discover the richness of Calabrian cuisine, characterized by its rustic simplicity and the use of locally sourced ingredients. From mouthwatering dishes to traditional food festivals, immerse yourself in the culinary traditions that define this region. Additionally, explore the delightful wines and spirits that complement the Calabrian dining experience.

Introduction to Calabrian Cuisine

Calabrian cuisine is a reflection of the region's rich agricultural heritage and the culinary traditions that have been cherished and passed down through generations. Located in the southernmost part of Italy, Calabria is surrounded by the azure waters of the Mediterranean Sea, which has played a significant role in shaping its cuisine. Furthermore, the region's historical connections with diverse cultures, including Greeks, Romans, Byzantines, Arabs, and Normans, have left a lasting impact on its culinary landscape.

One of the defining characteristics of Calabrian cuisine is its emphasis on using fresh, seasonal ingredients that are abundant in the region. The fertile soil, favorable climate, and proximity to the sea provide an abundant supply of produce, seafood, and aromatic herbs. Calabrians take great pride in sourcing their ingredients locally, resulting in dishes that burst with flavors and showcase the natural bounty of the land and sea.

The cuisine of Calabria is known for its vibrant and bold flavors, often described as robust and intense. The abundant use of chili peppers, particularly the famous Calabrian chili pepper or 'Peperoncino,' adds a fiery kick to many dishes. It infuses a distinct spiciness that sets Calabrian cuisine apart from other Italian regional cuisines. Whether it's incorporated into sauces, sausages, or spreads like 'Nduja, the chili pepper is an essential ingredient that adds depth and character to Calabrian dishes.

Seafood plays a prominent role in Calabrian cuisine, owing to its coastal location. Freshly caught fish, shellfish, and crustaceans feature prominently in dishes such as 'Pesce Spada alla ghiotta' (Swordfish with Tomato and Capers) or 'Calamari Ripieni' (Stuffed Calamari). The coastal towns and fishing villages along the Tyrrhenian and Ionian coasts offer a wealth of seafood delicacies that are savored by both locals and visitors.

In addition to seafood, Calabria's cuisine showcases the region's agricultural prowess. Local ingredients like the renowned 'Cipolla di Tropea' (Tropea Red Onion), which is sweet and mild, find their way into various dishes, salads, and condiments. Other regional products, such as 'Soppressata Calabrese' (a spicy dry-cured salami) and 'Pecorino Crotonese' (a sheep's milk cheese), add depth and complexity to the flavor profiles of Calabrian cuisine.

The culinary traditions of Calabria are preserved through family recipes and time-honored techniques. Many dishes are prepared using traditional methods, such as slow-cooking and braising, which allow flavors to meld and develop over time. The art of preserving food is also prominent in Calabrian cuisine, with sun-drying, pickling, and fermenting techniques employed to extend the shelf life of seasonal ingredients and create unique flavors.

Calabrian cuisine is a celebration of the region's natural abundance, historical influences, and the love and pride that the people of Calabria have for their culinary heritage. It is an invitation to savor the vibrant flavors, indulge in the harmonious blend of tastes, and experience the unique gastronomic journey that Calabria has to offer.

Must-Try Dishes and Local Ingredients

Calabria is renowned for its diverse and delectable range of signature dishes that will satisfy the palates of food enthusiasts. Prepare to indulge in a culinary adventure as you discover the unique flavors and ingredients that make Calabrian cuisine so remarkable.

One iconic dish that captures the essence of Calabrian cuisine is 'Nduja. This fiery spreadable salami is a true explosion of flavors, thanks to the Calabrian chili peppers used in its preparation. The spicy and smoky notes of 'Nduja create a tantalizing taste experience, making it a beloved ingredient in various dishes. Spread it on crusty bread, toss it into pasta, or use it to enhance the flavor of sauces and stews.

Another culinary gem from Calabria is the famous 'Cipolla di Tropea.' These sweet red onions, grown in the region's fertile soil, are known for their distinct flavor and versatility in the kitchen. The 'Cipolla di Tropea' adds a delightful touch to both cooked and raw dishes, imparting a mild sweetness and a subtle hint of tang. Enjoy them in salads, roasted alongside meats, or caramelized to create a luscious accompaniment to various recipes.

For pasta lovers, 'Pasta alla Norma' is a must-try dish that embodies the essence of Calabrian flavors. This classic pasta dish originates from Catania, Sicily, but is widely embraced in Calabria due to its incredible taste. The combination of al dente pasta, tender chunks of eggplant, rich tomato sauce, and crumbled ricotta salata cheese creates a harmonious blend of flavors and textures. Named after the opera by Bellini, 'Pasta alla Norma' is a celebration of Mediterranean ingredients and culinary artistry.

In addition to these signature dishes, Calabria boasts a plethora of other mouthwatering culinary treasures. Delight your taste buds with 'Soppressata Calabrese,' a traditional dry-cured salami with a bold and savory profile. Indulge in 'Scaloppine al Marsala,' a delicious veal dish cooked in Marsala wine and savory herbs. Experience the rustic charm of 'Pitta 'mpigliata,' a traditional Calabrian dessert made with dried figs, almonds, honey, and spices. These are just a few examples of the many incredible dishes that await you in Calabria.

As you continue your culinary exploration of Calabria, be prepared to encounter a diverse array of dishes that highlight the region's bountiful ingredients and traditional cooking techniques. Let your taste buds be tantalized by the following culinary delights:

'Fileja Calabresi': This handmade pasta is a staple in Calabrian cuisine. It is traditionally made by rolling and twisting small pieces of dough around a thin rod, creating a corkscrew shape. 'Fileja Calabresi' pairs perfectly with hearty meat or vegetable sauces, allowing you to savor the combination of flavors and textures.

'Baccalà alla Catanese': This dish features salted cod, which is soaked to remove the excess salt and then cooked with tomatoes, onions, capers, olives, and aromatic herbs. The result is a flavorful and succulent fish dish that showcases the region's affinity for seafood and bold seasonings.

'Sardella': A piquant and intensely flavored spread, 'Sardella' is made by blending salted anchovies, breadcrumbs, chili peppers, garlic, and olive oil. It is typically served as a condiment, adding a spicy kick to bruschetta, grilled vegetables, or pasta dishes.

'Cuzzupe': These traditional Easter sweet breads are shaped like various figures, such as crosses, doves, or lambs. They are made with a rich dough flavored with citrus zest and often adorned with colorful sprinkles or hard-boiled eggs. 'Cuzzupe' are a delightful treat enjoyed during festive occasions.

'Pezzente': A rustic and hearty dish, 'Pezzente' consists of slow-cooked pork or lamb, seasoned with fragrant herbs and spices. The meat is simmered until tender, resulting in a flavorful and comforting meal that showcases the region's affinity for slow-cooked meats.

'Tartufo di Pizzo': Indulge in the famous Calabrian dessert, 'Tartufo di Pizzo.' This delightful treat features a ball of creamy gelato, typically chocolate and hazelnut, coated in a chocolate shell and dusted with cocoa powder. It is the perfect way to satisfy your sweet tooth while enjoying the cool refreshment of gelato.

Throughout your culinary journey in Calabria, you will not only experience the flavors of the region but also witness the dedication and passion of the local artisans who meticulously craft these dishes. Whether you are exploring traditional trattorias, visiting local markets, or attending food festivals, the gastronomic offerings of Calabria will leave a lasting impression and create cherished memories of the region's culinary delights.

Traditional Food Festivals and Markets

Immerse yourself in the lively atmosphere of Calabria's traditional food festivals and markets, where you can experience the vibrant culinary culture firsthand. One notable event that showcases Calabria's love for spicy flavors is the "Sagra del Peperoncino" (Chili Pepper Festival) in Diamante. This annual festival celebrates the region's affinity for chili peppers, which are a staple ingredient in many Calabrian dishes. As you wander through the festival, you'll be tantalized by the aromas of sizzling peppers and various chili-infused delicacies. From fiery spreads and sauces to chili-infused oils and dried peppers, the festival offers a range of products for those who appreciate a bit of heat in their cuisine.

In addition to food festivals, Calabria is home to bustling markets that are a treasure trove for food enthusiasts. Catanzaro's "Mercato del Pesce" (Fish Market) is a vibrant hub where you can immerse yourself in the sights and sounds of fishermen unloading their daily catches. The market showcases an impressive array of seafood, from freshly caught fish and shellfish to succulent prawns and squid. It's a haven for seafood lovers who can choose from an abundance of ingredients to create their own culinary masterpieces.

Reggio Calabria's "Mercato di Via Demetrio Tripepi" is another must-visit market, known for its wide selection of fresh produce, local specialties, and culinary treasures. Strolling through the market's colorful stalls, you'll find an assortment of fruits, vegetables, aromatic herbs, and cheeses that reflect the region's agricultural abundance. Don't miss the opportunity to sample Calabria's renowned products like the 'Cipolla di Tropea,' the region's prized sweet red onions, or 'Nduja, the spicy spreadable salami that is a true Calabrian delicacy. The market offers a chance to interact with local vendors, who are passionate about their products and are always eager to share their knowledge and recommendations.

These traditional food festivals and markets in Calabria are more than just places to buy and taste local products. They offer a truly immersive experience that allows you to engage with the local culture and gain a deeper understanding of the region's culinary traditions.

At the "Sagra del Peperoncino" in Diamante, you'll not only have the chance to savor spicy dishes but also witness lively performances, music, and dancing that create a festive ambiance. Local artisans often showcase their handmade crafts, including pottery, artwork, and traditional souvenirs, adding to the vibrant atmosphere of the festival. You can engage in conversations with the locals, who are proud to share their knowledge of chili pepper cultivation, traditional recipes, and the significance of this ingredient in Calabrian cuisine.

As you venture into the bustling markets, such as the "Mercato del Pesce" in Catanzaro or the "Mercato di Via Demetrio Tripepi" in Reggio Calabria, the sensory overload of sights, sounds, and aromas will envelop you. The colorful displays of fresh produce, ranging from ripe tomatoes and fragrant basil to luscious figs and juicy oranges, are a testament to the region's fertile soil and agricultural diversity. The market vendors, often local farmers themselves, are eager to share stories about their products, offering insights into traditional farming practices and regional specialties.

Interacting with the vendors is an opportunity to learn about the traditional techniques and flavors that have been passed down through generations. You can engage in friendly conversations, seek cooking tips, or even discover hidden gems—unique ingredients or local delicacies that might not be found in mainstream supermarkets. The markets also provide an excellent chance to witness the art of haggling and the lively banter between customers and vendors, adding an element of excitement and authenticity to your experience.

Beyond the culinary delights, these festivals and markets also offer glimpses into Calabria's rich cultural heritage. Traditional music performances, folk dances, and cultural exhibitions often take place, showcasing the region's artistic traditions and folklore. You may encounter artisans crafting traditional musical instruments, creating intricate lacework, or demonstrating the art of traditional weaving.

By immersing yourself in the lively atmosphere of Calabria's food festivals and markets, you'll not only satisfy your taste buds but also forge a connection with the local community, experience the warmth of Calabrian hospitality, and create lasting memories of a region that truly cherishes its culinary traditions.

Wine and Spirits of Calabria

Calabria's exceptional wines and spirits perfectly complement the region's rich cuisine, offering a delightful sensory experience. With its diverse wine production, Calabria has gained recognition for its remarkable varieties, each with its own distinct characteristics and flavors.

One of the notable wines of Calabria is the robust red wine of Cirò. This wine is crafted from the native Gaglioppo grape, which thrives in the region's sun-drenched vineyards. Cirò wines are known for their deep red color, full body, and complex flavors that range from cherry and blackberry to hints of spices and earthiness. They pair wonderfully with the hearty and savory dishes of Calabria, enhancing the overall dining experience.

For those who prefer white wines, Calabria offers the crisp and refreshing Greco di Bianco. Made from the Greco Bianco grape variety, these wines exhibit vibrant acidity, citrus notes, and floral aromas. They are often enjoyed as aperitifs or paired with seafood and lighter fare, adding a touch of elegance to the dining experience.

To indulge in a sweet finale, Calabria presents the exquisite Moscato Passito di Saracena. This luscious dessert wine is produced in the hills of Saracena, where the Moscato Bianco grapes are left to dry on the vine, concentrating their sugars and flavors. The resulting wine is golden in color, with intense aromas of ripe fruits, honey, and floral undertones. Sipping on Moscato Passito di Saracena is a true indulgence, perfect for pairing with desserts or enjoyed on its own as a luxurious treat.

In addition to wines, Calabria offers traditional liqueurs that reflect the region's ancient herbal traditions. One such liqueur is Vecchio Amaro del Capo, a beloved herbal digestif. This bittersweet liqueur is crafted from a secret blend of herbs and botanicals, carefully selected for their aromatic and medicinal properties. Vecchio Amaro del Capo is often enjoyed as a digestive after meals, believed to aid digestion and invigorate the senses. Its herbal profile and rich flavors make it a unique and distinctive beverage, allowing you to immerse yourself in Calabria's cultural heritage.

Furthermore, Calabria's wine production extends beyond Cirò, Greco di Bianco, and Moscato Passito di Saracena, offering a range of other noteworthy varietals that showcase the region's viticultural prowess. Among these is the Gaglioppo-based wine, Magliocco, which delivers a medium-bodied red with velvety tannins and notes of black fruits and spices.

Another standout red wine is the Calabrese, also known as Calabria's "Chianti." This wine is crafted from a blend of indigenous grape varieties, including Gaglioppo, Greco Nero, and Nerello Cappuccio. Calabrese wines exhibit a good structure, balanced acidity, and a bouquet of ripe red fruits, making them a delightful companion to pasta dishes and grilled meats.

For white wine enthusiasts, Calabria offers the vibrant and aromatic white wine known as Pecorello. Made from the Pecorello grape, this wine showcases bright acidity, citrus flavors, and herbaceous undertones. It pairs excellently with seafood dishes, light salads, and fresh cheeses.

Moving beyond wine, Calabria presents a selection of traditional spirits that provide a glimpse into the region's cultural heritage. One such spirit is Amaro del Capo, a bitter liqueur made from a blend of local herbs, roots, and citrus peels. Amaro del Capo is often enjoyed as an aperitif or digestif, either neat or mixed into refreshing cocktails, and its complex flavors offer a delightful balance of bitterness, sweetness, and herbal nuances.

Limoncello, a well-known Italian liqueur, also holds a special place in Calabria's spirits repertoire. Made from the zest of locally grown lemons, Limoncello is cherished for its vibrant yellow color, zesty aroma, and invigorating citrus taste.

Served chilled, it serves as a delightful palate cleanser and a refreshing way to conclude a meal.

Whether indulging in the diverse wines or savoring the distinct flavors of traditional liqueurs, Calabria's exceptional beverages add depth and authenticity to the overall culinary experience. They provide a taste of the region's terroir, cultural heritage, and the passion of its winemakers and distillers. Exploring these wines and spirits in Calabria allows you to truly immerse yourself in the flavors and traditions that make this hidden gem of Italy an extraordinary destination for gastronomic discovery.

By exploring the culinary delights of Calabria, you will gain a deeper understanding of the region's cultural heritage and the importance of food in its identity. From simple and hearty dishes to unique local ingredients and beverages, Calabria's cuisine will leave an indelible mark on your taste buds and memories of this enchanting region.

Chapter 5: Natural Wonders and Outdoor Adventures

Sila National Park

Sila National Park, nestled in the heart of Calabria, is a true natural paradise that enchants visitors with its pristine beauty and diverse ecosystems. Spanning a vast area, the park is characterized by its striking mountain range, dense forests, and captivating lakes, creating a haven for outdoor enthusiasts and nature lovers alike.

As you step into Sila National Park, you'll find yourself immersed in a world of awe-inspiring landscapes. The majestic mountain range stands tall, its peaks reaching towards the sky, creating a dramatic backdrop against the horizon. The mountains are cloaked in verdant forests that showcase a rich tapestry of flora, with towering trees, colorful wildflowers, and vibrant foliage that changes with the seasons. Walking through the forested trails, you'll be captivated by the fresh scent of pine and the gentle rustling of leaves, creating a tranquil and rejuvenating atmosphere.

One of the highlights of Sila National Park is its collection of picturesque lakes that dot the region. These glistening bodies of water, such as Lake Arvo and Lake Ampollino, are nestled amidst the mountains, reflecting the surrounding natural splendor. The calm waters mirror the serene surroundings, creating a breathtaking sight that is both peaceful and mesmerizing. Whether you choose to leisurely stroll along the shores or indulge in water activities like kayaking or fishing, the lakes of Sila offer a serene respite from the outside world.

For outdoor adventurers, Sila National Park presents a wealth of activities to engage in. Hiking and trekking trails crisscross the park, allowing you to explore its hidden corners and discover its hidden gems. As you ascend the mountain trails, you'll be rewarded with panoramic vistas that stretch as far as the eye can see, offering glimpses of the lush valleys below and the distant sea shimmering on the horizon.

Wildlife enthusiasts will be delighted by the diverse array of animal species that call Sila home. The park's forests and meadows provide habitats for a wide range of wildlife, including the elusive Apennine wolf, deer, wild boars, and an assortment of bird species. With patience and a keen eye, you may catch glimpses of these enchanting creatures as they navigate their natural habitats.

Sila National Park truly caters to every outdoor pursuit, whether you seek thrilling adventures or serene moments of connection with nature. It is a place where you can embark on invigorating hikes, relish in the tranquility of the lakeside, and marvel at the unspoiled beauty that surrounds you. With its pristine landscapes and abundant recreational opportunities, Sila National Park beckons travelers to immerse themselves in its natural wonders and create lasting memories in this idyllic corner of Calabria.

Hiking and Trekking Trails:

The park boasts an extensive network of well-maintained hiking and trekking trails, catering to all levels of experience. Whether you're a seasoned hiker or a beginner, Sila National Park has a trail for you. With its diverse range of trails, you can embark on a hiking adventure that suits your fitness level and time constraints.

As you venture into Sila National Park, you'll find yourself surrounded by a captivating natural environment. The dense forests, characterized by towering pines and beech trees, create a serene atmosphere and provide shade during your hike. The trails wind their way through this verdant landscape, offering a cool and refreshing escape from the summer heat.

Meandering rivers and streams crisscross the park, adding to the enchanting ambiance. You may come across picturesque waterfalls along your hiking journey, their cascading waters creating a soothing soundtrack as you traverse the trails. Take a moment to pause and appreciate the natural beauty surrounding you.

Panoramic viewpoints are scattered throughout the park, offering breathtaking vistas of the sprawling landscapes. From these vantage points, you can marvel at the undulating hills, deep valleys, and distant mountains that stretch as far as the eye can see. The beauty of Sila National Park is truly awe-inspiring, and these viewpoints provide the perfect opportunity to capture memorable photographs or simply soak in the awe-inspiring scenery.

One highlight of hiking in Sila National Park is the opportunity to summit Mount Botte Donato, the highest peak in Sila. This challenging but rewarding hike takes you to an elevation of over 1,900 meters (6,230 feet) and rewards you with sweeping vistas of the surrounding landscape. As you reach the summit, you'll be treated to panoramic views that showcase the park's vastness and the majestic beauty of Calabria's natural surroundings.

Throughout your hike in Sila National Park, you'll have the opportunity to witness the rich biodiversity that thrives within its boundaries. The park is home to a variety of plant and animal species, adding to the allure of your hiking experience.

As you traverse the trails, keep an eye out for the diverse flora that graces the park's landscape. Towering trees, such as the majestic silver fir and Calabrian black pine, dominate the forest canopy. These ancient trees not only provide shade but also serve as habitats for a plethora of wildlife. Look closer, and you'll discover a vibrant tapestry of wildflowers, including orchids, daisies, and vibrant heathers that add splashes of color to the green surroundings.

Sila National Park is a haven for animal lovers and wildlife enthusiasts. The forested areas are teeming with life, with a variety of animal species making their homes here. If you're lucky, you might spot the elusive Apennine wolf gracefully maneuvering through the forest, or come across a family of wild boars foraging for food. Keep your eyes and ears open for the energetic red squirrel as it scampers through the treetops.

Birdwatchers will be delighted by the avian inhabitants of Sila National Park. The park is a paradise for birdlife, attracting a wide range of species. Listen for the melodic song of the Eurasian blackbird or the distinctive call of the great spotted woodpecker. With patience and a keen eye, you might catch sight of the majestic golden eagle soaring through the sky or spot a group of colorful hoopoes with their distinct crown of feathers.

As you hike to the summit of Mount Botte Donato, you'll traverse varying ecosystems, witnessing the gradual changes in vegetation and wildlife. The higher you climb, the more you'll encounter alpine meadows dotted with delicate wildflowers and resilient plants adapted to the harsher conditions of higher elevations. Be on the lookout for mountain-dwelling creatures such as chamois and foxes, which have adapted to survive in these rugged environments.

Sila National Park's hiking trails offer not only a physical challenge but also a journey of discovery. Along the way, you'll immerse yourself in the natural wonders of Calabria, witnessing the interconnectedness of flora and fauna and gaining a deeper appreciation for the delicate balance of the ecosystem.

Remember to hike responsibly, respecting the park's rules and regulations, and leaving no trace of your presence. By doing so, you'll ensure that future generations can continue to enjoy the pristine beauty of Sila National Park and its remarkable biodiversity.

So, lace up your hiking boots, grab your backpack, and prepare for an unforgettable adventure through the diverse landscapes and remarkable wildlife of Sila National Park in Calabria's hidden gem.

Wildlife Spotting:

Sila National Park is a haven for wildlife enthusiasts and animal lovers, offering a rich diversity of species that thrive within its protected boundaries. As you explore the park's pristine landscapes, keep your senses attuned to the movements and sounds of the natural world, for there are numerous remarkable creatures to discover.

One of the most iconic and elusive animals found in Sila National Park is the Apennine wolf. These majestic predators, known for their intelligence and adaptability, roam the park's forests in search of prey. While catching a glimpse of these wolves can be challenging due to their stealthy nature, the possibility of encountering them adds an air of excitement to any visit.

As you traverse the park's trails and meander through the woodlands, keep an eye out for wild boars. These robust and agile creatures, with their distinctive snouts and tusks, are a common sight in Sila. They play an essential role in shaping the ecosystem through their foraging habits, and observing them in their natural habitat is a memorable experience.

Another notable resident of Sila National Park is the red deer. These graceful and majestic creatures can often be spotted grazing in meadows or moving silently through the forests. Their striking appearance and regal presence add to the park's natural beauty, providing a glimpse into the harmonious coexistence of wildlife and wilderness.

For those with a love for avian wonders, Sila National Park offers a captivating array of bird species. Look to the skies and treetops for the sight of the majestic golden eagle, soaring high with its impressive wingspan. The park's varied habitats provide a habitat for diverse birdlife, including the black woodpecker, known for its distinct drumming sounds and intricate plumage. Birdwatchers will also have the opportunity to spot the peregrine falcon, renowned for its incredible speed and agility, as well as the tawny owl, which emerges at dusk, filling the air with its haunting hoots.

In addition to these notable species, Sila National Park is home to a host of smaller mammals that contribute to the park's biodiversity. Look for the quick and agile foxes as they dart through the underbrush, or the charming hares as they bound across open meadows. Squirrels, with their bushy tails and acrobatic antics, can be spotted scurrying among the trees, adding a touch of liveliness to the park's serene atmosphere.

As you explore Sila National Park, it's important to remember that wildlife encounters require patience, respect, and a deep appreciation for the natural world. Keep in mind that the park's wildlife is wild and should be observed from a distance to ensure their safety and well-being.

Beyond the iconic species mentioned, Sila National Park is also home to a variety of other fascinating animals. If you're lucky, you might come across the tracks or signs of elusive creatures such as the European wildcat, a secretive feline known for its solitary nature. These elusive cats are skilled hunters and masters of camouflage, making them a true gem to spot in the wild.

The park's woodlands and meadows are teeming with life, and the diligent observer may catch a glimpse of small mammals such as badgers, known for their nocturnal habits and distinctive markings. These nocturnal creatures are primarily active at night, but with a bit of luck, you might spot one during the early morning or at dusk.

Sila National Park is a paradise for birdwatchers, with its varied habitats attracting an impressive range of avian species. Look for the striking Eurasian hoopoe with its distinctive crest and vibrant plumage, or listen for the melodious songs of the blackcap, a small passerine bird known for its beautiful vocalizations. If you're near the park's water sources, keep an eye out for the elegant grey heron, often seen standing still near rivers or lakes as it patiently hunts for fish.

During your time in Sila National Park, make sure to observe the wildlife with minimal disruption to their natural behavior. Keep noise levels to a minimum, avoid feeding the animals, and always follow park guidelines and regulations to preserve the delicate balance of the ecosystem.

Remember that wildlife encounters are a privilege, and the ability to witness these remarkable creatures in their natural habitats is a humbling experience. By being respectful stewards of the park and its inhabitants, you contribute to the preservation of Sila National Park's biodiversity for future generations to appreciate and cherish.

So, as you explore Sila National Park's breathtaking landscapes, be prepared to be captivated by the diverse array of wildlife that calls this pristine region home. Keep your eyes and ears open, and with a dash of luck and patience, you'll create memories of unforgettable encounters with the enchanting creatures of Sila National Park.

Sila's Lakes:

The park's enchanting lakes are among its most captivating features, adding a touch of serenity and beauty to the already stunning surroundings. One of the must-visit lakes in Sila National Park is Lake Arvo, a tranquil body of water that exudes a sense of calm and tranquility. As you take a leisurely stroll along its shores, you'll be immersed in the peaceful ambiance created by the gentle lapping of the water and the soothing sounds of nature. The lake is embraced by verdant landscapes, with lush forests and rolling hills that enhance its natural allure. Capture the breathtaking scenery with your camera or simply take a moment to soak in the picturesque surroundings.

Another gem within Sila National Park is Lake Ampollino, nestled amidst the majestic mountains. This lake offers not only mesmerizing views but also a range of water-based activities for adventure enthusiasts. Rent a kayak or a canoe and explore the pristine waters, gliding along as you take in the panoramic vistas that unfold before you. Fishing enthusiasts will find joy in casting their lines into the clear waters, hoping for a catch of trout or perch. The tranquil ambiance and idyllic setting make Lake Ampollino an ideal spot for a leisurely picnic. Spread out a blanket, savor local delicacies, and revel in the serenity that surrounds you.

As you bask in the serenity of these pristine natural wonders, you'll find yourself immersed in an atmosphere of tranquility and rejuvenation. The lakes of Sila National Park provide a respite from the demands of daily life, allowing you to unwind and appreciate the beauty of the surrounding landscapes.

Lake Arvo, with its tranquil waters, offers a perfect setting for reflection and relaxation. Take a leisurely stroll along its shores, feeling the gentle breeze caress your face and listening to the symphony of birdsong. The verdant landscapes that encircle the lake create a picturesque backdrop, adding to its enchanting allure. You may choose to find a secluded spot to sit and meditate, or simply sit on a bench and admire the captivating vistas that unfold before your eyes.

On the other hand, Lake Ampollino presents a more dynamic and adventurous experience. Nestled amidst the mountains, this picturesque lake invites you to partake in a range of water-based activities. Glide across the pristine waters in a kayak or canoe, feeling the cool mist on your skin as you navigate through the serene surroundings. The towering peaks and lush forests that surround the lake create a dramatic panorama, immersing you in nature's grandeur. Fishing enthusiasts can cast their lines into the lake, testing their skills and patience as they seek to catch a prized fish. As you engage in these activities, the sense of freedom and connection with nature will invigorate your spirit.

Both lakes offer ideal spots for a leisurely picnic. Spread out a blanket on the grassy shores, indulge in delicious local delicacies, and savor the moment. The calm ambiance and breathtaking vistas provide the perfect backdrop for a memorable dining experience. Allow yourself to be captivated by the interplay of light and shadows on the water's surface, as the lakes mirror the beauty of the sky and the surrounding landscape.

Whether you prefer a tranquil walk around Lake Arvo or an adventurous exploration of Lake Ampollino, the lakes of Sila National Park beckon you to escape into a realm of natural splendor. These enchanting bodies of water not only enhance the park's allure but also offer moments of tranquility, inspiration, and appreciation for the wonders of the natural world.

Aspromonte National Park:

Aspromonte National Park, situated in the southernmost part of Calabria, is a true haven for nature enthusiasts and adventurers seeking an authentic and captivating wilderness experience. This mountainous region offers a rugged and untamed beauty that is sure to leave a lasting impression on anyone who visits.

The park's landscape is characterized by towering mountains, deep valleys, and sweeping vistas that stretch as far as the eye can see. The rugged terrain and jagged peaks of Aspromonte create a dramatic backdrop for exploration and discovery. As you traverse its trails and paths, you'll be immersed in a world of awe-inspiring vistas and breathtaking panoramas.

Ancient forests blanket the slopes of Aspromonte, adding to its mystical allure. These forests are a testament to the enduring power of nature, with trees that have stood tall for centuries. Among the verdant foliage, you'll find a rich diversity of plant life, including ancient chestnut trees, beech forests, and an array of aromatic herbs. The air is perfumed with the scents of nature, and the symphony of birdsong fills the tranquil atmosphere.

The biodiversity within Aspromonte National Park is truly remarkable. It serves as a sanctuary for numerous animal species, both large and small. Wildlife enthusiasts will have the opportunity to encounter elusive creatures such as the majestic Apennine wolf, wild boars, and the agile chamois. Additionally, the park is home to various bird species, including raptors like the golden eagle and peregrine falcon. The rich tapestry of flora and fauna in Aspromonte is a testament to the region's ecological significance and its commitment to preserving its natural heritage.

Exploring Aspromonte National Park offers a multitude of adventures and experiences. Hiking through its trails will lead you to hidden valleys, crystal-clear mountain streams, and cascading waterfalls that provide moments of tranquility and reflection. The park's summits offer breathtaking panoramic views, allowing you to witness the sheer grandeur of the surrounding landscape.

For those seeking a deeper understanding of the park's natural wonders, guided excursions and nature walks are available. Accompanied by knowledgeable experts, you'll learn about the park's history, geology, and the delicate balance between human settlements and the pristine environment. You may have the chance to visit traditional villages that have retained their unique character and witness the harmonious coexistence between locals and the natural world.

Aspromonte National Park is a testament to the raw beauty and resilience of Calabria's natural landscapes. Its rugged mountains, ancient forests, and rich biodiversity offer a captivating experience for nature enthusiasts and adventurers alike. Prepare to be enchanted by the untamed beauty of Aspromonte as you immerse yourself in its timeless allure and uncover the secrets that lie within its wilderness.

Exploring the Wild Aspromonte Mountains:

Embark on an unforgettable adventure through the untamed landscapes of the Aspromonte Mountains, where nature reigns supreme. This majestic mountain range is a haven for outdoor enthusiasts, offering a plethora of trails that wind their way through dense forests, along rushing rivers, and up to breathtaking summits.

As you set foot on the trails of Aspromonte, you'll find yourself immersed in a world of natural wonders. The dense forests envelop you in their green embrace, creating a sense of serenity and seclusion. Tall trees sway in the gentle breeze, their leaves whispering secrets of the ancient wilderness that surrounds you.

As you venture deeper into the mountains, the sound of cascading waterfalls fills the air. These magnificent natural formations create a symphony of rushing water, captivating your senses and inviting you to pause and appreciate their beauty. Take a moment to breathe in the crisp mountain air and feel the mist on your face as you witness the raw power and elegance of nature.

The trails in Aspromonte cater to all levels of hikers, from those seeking a challenging adventure to those looking for a leisurely walk immersed in nature's splendor. If you're up for a demanding hike, tackle the steep ascents that lead to the highest peaks, where you'll be rewarded with awe-inspiring panoramic views stretching as far as the eye can see. Gaze upon the vast expanse of the mountains, the rolling hills, and the picturesque valleys below, and feel a sense of accomplishment and wonder wash over you.

For those preferring a more leisurely pace, meandering paths offer a tranquil journey through the mountains. Wander alongside babbling streams, breathe in the fragrant aromas of wildflowers, and listen to the melodic chirping of birds perched on branches above. These serene walks provide an opportunity to immerse yourself fully in the natural rhythms of Aspromonte, allowing you to forge a deep connection with the environment and rejuvenate your spirit.

No matter which trail you choose, the Aspromonte Mountains promise unforgettable views and a sense of awe that resonates within your soul. The untouched beauty of this untamed wilderness is a testament to the power and grandeur of nature. It is a place where you can escape the chaos of everyday life and find solace in the simplicity and magnificence of the natural world.

Feel the exhilaration as you conquer challenging inclines and navigate rocky terrain. The rugged beauty of Aspromonte's peaks beckons to the intrepid explorer within you, offering a sense of accomplishment and an opportunity to push your limits. Stand atop a summit, with the wind tousling your hair and panoramic vistas stretching before you, and revel in the awe-inspiring views that reward your efforts.

But Aspromonte is not just about conquering heights; it is also a place of tranquility and introspection. Take leisurely walks along gentle paths, allowing yourself to be enveloped by the peaceful ambiance of the mountains. The rhythmic sounds of nature accompany your every step, creating a soothing symphony of birdsong, rustling leaves, and distant rustling streams. Allow yourself to be fully present in these moments, letting the tranquility of Aspromonte wash away the stresses of daily life.

Throughout your journey, you'll encounter an incredible diversity of flora and fauna. The mountains are adorned with a tapestry of vibrant wildflowers, from delicate alpine blossoms to hardy mountain herbs. Listen to the rustling of leaves and twigs underfoot, for it may reveal the presence of elusive wildlife. Keep your eyes peeled for glimpses of graceful deer, playful foxes, or the agile chamois gracefully traversing the slopes. Aspromonte is a sanctuary for these creatures, and their presence reminds us of the delicate balance that exists between humans and the natural world.

As you traverse the trails of Aspromonte, take time to pause and immerse yourself in the serenity of hidden valleys, secluded waterfalls, and pristine alpine lakes. Dip your hands into crystal-clear streams, taste the purity of the mountain water, and let the coolness invigorate your senses. Find solace in the simplicity of nature, far removed from the complexities of modern life.

Whether you're a seasoned hiker seeking an adrenaline-pumping adventure or a nature lover craving a peaceful communion with the great outdoors, the Aspromonte Mountains offer an experience that resonates deep within your being. This untamed wilderness, with its awe-inspiring views, diverse ecosystems, and captivating trails, has the power to ignite your sense of wonder, inspire self-discovery, and leave an indelible imprint on your soul.

So, step into the untamed landscapes of Aspromonte, where nature's beauty knows no bounds. Allow the mountains to guide you on a journey of exploration, self-reflection, and connection with the natural world. The Aspromonte Mountains await your arrival, ready to unleash their transformative power and leave you with memories that will last a lifetime.

Flora and Fauna:

Aspromonte National Park is a haven of biodiversity, boasting an impressive array of plant and animal species that thrive within its boundaries. The park's diverse ecosystems create a habitat that supports a rich and varied plant life, captivating nature enthusiasts and botany enthusiasts alike.

The park's forests are adorned with ancient chestnut trees, some of which have stood tall for centuries, lending an air of mystique and enchantment to the landscape. These majestic trees provide shade and shelter to a multitude of flora and fauna, creating a vibrant and interconnected ecosystem. Beech forests, with their dense foliage and towering trees, add to the park's natural splendor, offering a cool respite during hot summer months.

One of the highlights of Aspromonte's flora is the elusive Calabrian fir (Abies nebrodensis), a rare and protected tree species found exclusively within the region. This endemic fir, characterized by its slender silhouette and dark green needles, has faced the threat of extinction and is now carefully conserved within the park. Spotting a Calabrian fir during your explorations is a remarkable experience, as it symbolizes the resilience of nature and the park's commitment to preservation.

Wildlife enthusiasts will be delighted by the chance to encounter fascinating creatures that call Aspromonte National Park home. The park provides a sanctuary for elusive animals such as the wildcat, a secretive feline species known for its solitary nature. Patient observers may be rewarded with a glimpse of this enigmatic creature as it navigates its way through the dense vegetation.

Other notable residents of Aspromonte include wild boars, which roam freely in the park's forests, leaving traces of their presence through rooted soil and distinctive tracks. These robust mammals, with their imposing tusks and strong demeanor, embody the untamed spirit of the wilderness. Badgers, with their nocturnal habits and distinctive black and white markings, contribute to the park's diverse mammalian population.

Additionally, Aspromonte National Park is inhabited by various reptiles, adding to its ecological richness. Lizards, such as the European green lizard and the Italian wall lizard, can be spotted basking in the sun on rocks and fallen logs. Snake species like the Aesculapian snake and the dice snake quietly move through the underbrush, playing vital roles in maintaining the park's delicate balance.

In addition to the charismatic species mentioned, Aspromonte National Park is also home to a plethora of avian life, delighting birdwatchers and nature enthusiasts. The park serves as a haven for various bird species, both resident and migratory. Ornithologists and birdwatchers can observe the elegant flight of birds such as the peregrine falcon, which soars gracefully through the skies, and the tawny owl, known for its distinctive hooting during the night. The park's diverse habitats, ranging from dense forests to open meadows, provide nesting grounds and feeding areas for a wide range of bird species.

As you traverse the trails and delve deeper into the park's wilderness, you may also come across smaller creatures that contribute to the rich tapestry of Aspromonte's biodiversity. Keep an eye out for agile squirrels as they scamper along branches, displaying their acrobatic prowess. You may even spot hedgehogs or shrews foraging among fallen leaves, showcasing the park's thriving ecosystem at ground level.

Exploring Aspromonte National Park is not only an opportunity to witness the wonders of biodiversity but also a chance to learn about conservation efforts and the delicate balance between human interaction and preserving the natural environment. The park's educational programs and interpretive centers provide valuable insights into the importance of protecting these habitats and the steps taken to ensure the survival of its remarkable species.

Whether you find yourself captivated by the ancient chestnut trees, intrigued by the elusive Calabrian fir, or in awe of the diverse wildlife, Aspromonte National Park offers a truly immersive experience in the heart of Calabria's natural wonders. The encounters with its remarkable flora and fauna will leave you with a profound appreciation for the interconnectedness of all living things and the need to preserve these pristine environments for future generations to enjoy.

Excursions and Nature Walks:

The park offers a variety of guided excursions and nature walks, providing visitors with the opportunity to delve deeper into the wonders of Aspromonte National Park. Led by knowledgeable experts, these guided experiences are designed to enhance your understanding of the park's history, geology, and the diverse flora and fauna that call it home.

During these excursions, you'll have the chance to unravel the secrets of Aspromonte as experienced guides share their expertise and insights. They will provide fascinating information about the park's formation, geological features, and the ecological significance of its diverse ecosystems. Learn about the forces of nature that have shaped the mountains, valleys, and rivers, and gain a deeper appreciation for the geological processes that have contributed to the park's unique landscapes.

As you venture deeper into the park, your guides will introduce you to the remarkable plant and animal life that thrives within its boundaries. Discover the diverse flora, from ancient trees such as chestnuts and beeches to the vibrant array of wildflowers that carpet the meadows during the spring and summer months. Gain an understanding of the delicate balance of ecosystems and the vital role each species plays in maintaining the park's biodiversity.

One of the highlights of these guided excursions is the opportunity to explore hidden valleys that are off the beaten path. Venture into secluded areas that reveal a quieter side of Aspromonte, away from the more frequented trails. These hidden valleys often harbor unique plant species and provide havens for wildlife, offering a glimpse into the park's untouched beauty.

Additionally, guided excursions may include visits to traditional villages nestled within or near the park. These villages have preserved their cultural heritage and offer a glimpse into the traditional way of life in the region. Explore charming cobblestone streets, admire the architectural charm of centuries-old buildings, and interact with friendly locals who proudly share their customs and traditions.

During these encounters, you'll witness the harmonious coexistence between human settlements and the pristine natural environment. Gain an understanding of the symbiotic relationship between the local communities and the park, as residents have learned to live in harmony with nature, respecting and preserving the ecological integrity of the area.

By participating in these guided excursions and nature walks, you'll not only deepen your connection with Aspromonte but also contribute to its conservation efforts. The knowledgeable guides impart a sense of responsibility and stewardship, encouraging visitors to appreciate and protect the park's fragile ecosystems for future generations to enjoy.

These guided excursions and nature walks offer a wealth of enriching experiences that go beyond the surface level of exploration. As you walk alongside knowledgeable experts, you'll have the opportunity to engage in insightful discussions and ask questions, deepening your understanding of Aspromonte's intricate tapestry of natural and cultural heritage.

Guides will share captivating stories and anecdotes about the park's history, shedding light on the ancient civilizations that once inhabited these lands and the historical events that have shaped the region. Gain a sense of the deep-rooted connection between the local communities and the land, as well as the enduring traditions that have been passed down through generations.

Throughout your journey, you'll witness firsthand the incredible resilience of the flora and fauna that call Aspromonte home. Guides will point out the unique adaptations of plants and animals to the rugged mountain environment, highlighting the strategies they employ to thrive in this challenging habitat. Learn about the important role these species play in maintaining the delicate balance of the ecosystem and the conservation efforts in place to protect them.

The exploration of hidden valleys will take you to places of tranquility and seclusion, where the sounds of nature envelop you and the beauty of untouched landscapes unfolds before your eyes. These valleys often harbor hidden streams, cascading waterfalls, and serene clearings where you can pause to absorb the serenity of the surroundings. The guides will share their knowledge of the ecological significance of these valleys, offering insights into the delicate interplay of sunlight, water, and vegetation that sustains these hidden gems.

Visiting traditional villages within or near the park provides a unique window into the local way of life and cultural traditions. Immerse yourself in the warm hospitality of the villagers, who are eager to share their stories, customs, and artisanal crafts. Explore the narrow alleyways, visit ancient churches adorned with centuries-old frescoes, and savor traditional dishes that have been lovingly passed down through generations. These encounters provide a deeper appreciation for the profound connection between the local communities and the natural environment they coexist with.

As you conclude your guided excursions and nature walks, you'll depart with a profound sense of awe and reverence for Aspromonte National Park. The experiences shared with the knowledgeable guides will leave a lasting imprint, inspiring you to become an advocate for the preservation and conservation of this exceptional natural wonder. By embracing the wisdom and insights imparted during these journeys, you can play an active role in ensuring the continued protection of Aspromonte's extraordinary landscapes and the cultural heritage that resides within its boundaries.

Embark on these guided excursions and nature walks in Aspromonte National Park, where knowledge, appreciation, and conservation intertwine to create a truly immersive and transformative experience. Discover the secrets of the park, embrace the stories of its past and present, and forge a personal connection with the splendor of this natural paradise.

Chapter 6: Off the Beaten Path: Hidden Gems of Calabria

Gerace

Nestled amidst the rolling hills of Calabria, Gerace is a picturesque village that exudes a timeless charm. As visitors approach Gerace, they are immediately captivated by the village's idyllic setting. Surrounded by lush greenery and commanding panoramic views, Gerace offers a serene escape from the hustle and bustle of modern life.

Gerace's well-preserved medieval character is a testament to its rich history, making it a captivating destination for history enthusiasts and curious travelers alike. Walking through the cobblestone streets of Gerace feels like stepping back in time, as the village's medieval architecture transports visitors to a bygone era. The village's strategic position on a hilltop was once a defensive advantage, and remnants of ancient walls and fortifications can still be seen today.

This enchanting gem allows visitors to catch a glimpse of the region's fascinating history and architectural heritage. The influences of various civilizations that once thrived in Calabria are evident in Gerace's structures. The village showcases a harmonious blend of Norman, Gothic, and Byzantine architectural styles, resulting in a unique and captivating atmosphere.

One of the highlights of Gerace is its magnificent cathedral, a true architectural masterpiece. The Gerace Cathedral, dating back to the 11th century, stands as a testament to the village's religious and cultural significance. Its impressive facade and ornate details command attention, drawing visitors to explore its interior. Inside the cathedral, visitors are greeted by stunning mosaics, intricate frescoes, and ancient relics, each telling a story of Gerace's past.

Wandering through Gerace's narrow streets is an enchanting experience. The medieval houses, with their weathered stone facades and wooden balconies, create a sense of timelessness. Arched doorways, hidden courtyards, and charming squares add to the village's allure. As visitors explore the labyrinthine streets, they can't help but feel a connection to the generations of people who once called Gerace home.

For those with a passion for archaeology, the Gerace Antiquarium is a treasure trove of ancient artifacts. Housed within a former Capuchin monastery, this archaeological museum offers a fascinating insight into Gerace's past. The exhibits display a range of artifacts, including pottery, sculptures, and ancient Roman and Greek relics. Each artifact provides a window into the daily lives, customs, and beliefs of the ancient civilizations that once thrived in the region.

Gerace's picturesque setting, well-preserved medieval charm, and rich historical heritage make it a truly enchanting destination. Whether strolling through its streets, marveling at its cathedral, or delving into its ancient past at the Antiquarium, visitors to Gerace are transported to a different time and place. This hidden gem in Calabria invites exploration, discovery, and an appreciation for the region's remarkable history and architectural treasures.

Gerace Cathedral:

The imposing Gerace Cathedral stands proudly at the heart of the village, commanding attention with its remarkable grandeur and intricate details. Dating back to the 11th century, this architectural masterpiece has become an iconic symbol of Gerace and a testament to the rich history of the region.

As you approach the cathedral, you'll be struck by its impressive facade, which showcases a harmonious blend of architectural styles. The cathedral exhibits elements of Norman, Gothic, and Byzantine design, reflecting the influences of the various civilizations that have shaped Calabria over the centuries. This fusion of styles creates a visually captivating and unique structure that stands as a testament to the cultural heritage of the region.

Upon stepping inside the Gerace Cathedral, you'll find yourself immersed in a world of breathtaking beauty and religious significance. The interior is adorned with stunning mosaics that adorn the walls and ceilings, depicting scenes from biblical stories and saints. These intricate mosaics, crafted with meticulous attention to detail, are a testament to the skill and artistry of the craftsmen of the time.

In addition to the mosaics, the cathedral is also home to a remarkable collection of ancient relics. These sacred artifacts, ranging from ornate chalices to intricately carved statues, provide a glimpse into the religious traditions and practices of the past. Each relic holds its own historical and spiritual significance, adding to the aura of reverence within the cathedral.

One of the highlights of a visit to Gerace Cathedral is the opportunity to admire its awe-inspiring frescoes. These vibrant paintings, created by skilled artists centuries ago, adorn the walls and vaulted ceilings of the cathedral. The frescoes depict scenes from the life of Christ, biblical narratives, and saints, telling stories that have captivated visitors for generations.

Stepping into Gerace Cathedral is like stepping into a time capsule, where the rich history and spirituality of Calabria come to life. The grandeur of the architecture, the intricate mosaics, the sacred relics, and the mesmerizing frescoes all contribute to an atmosphere of wonder and reverence.

The cathedral's architectural details are a testament to the skill and craftsmanship of the artisans who contributed to its construction. The interplay of different architectural styles is evident throughout the cathedral's interior. The Norman influence can be seen in the sturdy columns and arches, while the Gothic elements manifest in the pointed arches and ribbed vaults that add height and elegance to the space. The Byzantine touch is evident in the intricate decorative motifs and the use of gold accents, creating a sense of opulence and spiritual transcendence.

As you wander through the cathedral, the play of light and shadow creates a mystical ambiance, further enhancing the spiritual experience. Sunlight filters through stained glass windows, casting vibrant hues and illuminating the space with a divine glow. The flickering candlelight adds an ethereal quality, creating a serene and contemplative atmosphere that invites introspection and reverence.

The cathedral also holds a rich history within its walls. It has witnessed countless religious ceremonies, celebrations, and important events throughout the centuries. From royal coronations to solemn religious processions, the cathedral has been a focal point of faith and community gathering.

Beyond its architectural and historical significance, Gerace Cathedral serves as a place of worship and pilgrimage. The faithful come to seek solace, offer prayers, and connect with their spiritual beliefs. The cathedral's sacredness permeates the air, fostering a sense of tranquility and reflection that is both soothing and awe-inspiring.

Visiting Gerace Cathedral is not just an architectural exploration; it is an immersive journey into the heart and soul of Calabria's religious and cultural heritage. It is a place where art, spirituality, and history converge, leaving visitors with a deep appreciation for the craftsmanship, devotion, and legacy of the people who built and maintained this sacred place.

Whether you are an architecture enthusiast, a history buff, or a seeker of spiritual experiences, Gerace Cathedral is a must-visit destination in Calabria. Its grandeur, intricate details, and profound ambiance make it a remarkable testament to the region's cultural richness and an unforgettable highlight of any exploration of this hidden gem of a village.

Medieval Streets and Architecture:

Exploring Gerace is like stepping into a storybook, where every corner reveals a glimpse of the village's fascinating history and architectural splendor. As you embark on a leisurely stroll through its narrow, winding streets, you'll find yourself immersed in a bygone era.

The village of Gerace boasts an exceptional preservation of its medieval buildings, showcasing the architectural styles and influences of the various civilizations that once thrived in the area. The centuries-old stone houses stand proudly, their weathered facades telling tales of generations past. The craftsmanship and attention to detail in the construction are evident in the ornate doorways, arched windows, and intricate carvings that adorn the buildings.

Wandering through Gerace, you'll encounter enchanting archways that beckon you to explore further. These ancient passages lead to hidden courtyards, offering peaceful retreats adorned with colorful flowers, trickling fountains, and inviting benches. Here, you can take a moment to rest and absorb the ambiance while marveling at the harmonious blend of nature and history.

The architecture of Gerace is a captivating tapestry that reflects the influences of diverse civilizations. The Norman, Gothic, and Byzantine styles seamlessly intertwine, creating a unique and captivating atmosphere. The Norman influence can be seen in the sturdy stone structures, while the Gothic elements are apparent in the pointed arches and soaring spires. Byzantine touches manifest in the intricately designed mosaics, adding a touch of opulence and grandeur.

As you wander through the village, you'll have the opportunity to admire the architectural treasures up close. Pay attention to the details etched into the stone facades, such as the delicate floral motifs, sculpted figures, and religious symbols. These intricate embellishments serve as testaments to the craftsmanship and devotion of the artisans who left their mark on Gerace.

The overall ambiance of Gerace is one of tranquility and timelessness. The absence of modern structures and the preservation of its medieval character transport visitors to a simpler era. With every step, you'll find yourself captivated by the village's undeniable charm and the palpable sense of history that permeates the air.

As you continue your leisurely stroll through Gerace, the immersive experience intensifies, drawing you deeper into the rich tapestry of its history and culture.

The narrow, winding streets of Gerace reveal surprises at every turn. Allow yourself to get lost in the labyrinthine alleys, where time seems to stand still. Each step unravels a new vista, with centuries-old stone houses lining the cobblestone streets. Their facades bear the marks of age, their weathered appearance a testament to the passage of time. You can't help but feel a sense of reverence as you walk among these architectural marvels, imagining the lives and stories that unfolded within their walls.

The archways of Gerace are like portals to another world, inviting you to venture deeper into its secrets. Passing through these arches, you enter hidden courtyards tucked away from the bustling streets. Here, you'll find a serene oasis where the sound of trickling fountains and the scent of blooming flowers fill the air. The hidden courtyards offer a glimpse into the daily lives of Gerace's residents, a space of respite and tranquility amidst the bustling medieval village.

The architectural influences that shaped Gerace are diverse and captivating. The village bears witness to the Norman conquerors who left their mark with their sturdy fortresses and defensive structures. The Gothic style, with its pointed arches and ribbed vaults, is prominent in Gerace's churches, lending an air of grandeur and spirituality. Byzantine influences can be seen in the intricate mosaics adorning the facades and interiors of religious buildings, their vibrant colors and geometric patterns mesmerizing visitors.

The interplay of these architectural styles creates a harmonious blend, resulting in Gerace's unique character. It's a testament to the resilience and adaptability of the village, as different civilizations left their imprints throughout the centuries. The architecture not only serves as a visual feast but also tells a story of Gerace's evolution, its transformation shaped by the ebb and flow of history.

As you meander through Gerace, take a moment to soak in the ambiance that surrounds you. Feel the weight of the past, the whispers of stories echoing through the narrow streets. The unique atmosphere of Gerace is a captivating blend of architectural wonders, inviting you to immerse yourself fully in its beauty and charm.

Exploring Gerace is a journey of discovery—an opportunity to step into the pages of history, to witness the architectural legacy of bygone eras, and to connect with the enduring spirit of this remarkable village. Embrace the sense of wonder as you traverse its medieval streets, for Gerace is more than just a collection of buildings—it's a living testament to the rich cultural heritage of Calabria.

Gerace Antiquarium:

For history enthusiasts, a visit to the Gerace Antiquarium is a must. Housed within a former Capuchin monastery, this archaeological museum offers a fascinating insight into Gerace's ancient past. As you step inside, you'll be transported back in time, surrounded by a collection of artifacts that tell the story of the region's rich cultural heritage.

The Gerace Antiquarium boasts an extensive collection of relics and objects that span centuries. Marvel at the intricately crafted pottery, which showcases the artistic skills of the ancient inhabitants of Gerace. Admire the delicate sculptures that provide a glimpse into the artistic traditions of the past. Among the highlights are the ancient Roman and Greek relics, which offer a deeper understanding of the historical connections and influences that shaped Gerace.

As you explore Gerace, don't forget to pause and take in the panoramic views of the surrounding countryside. The village is strategically located, offering breathtaking vistas of the rolling hills that stretch as far as the eye can see. The lush vineyards that blanket the landscape add a touch of vibrant green, creating a picturesque scene that captures the essence of Calabria. And on clear days, the sparkling Ionian Sea in the distance serves as a constant reminder of the region's coastal allure.

Gerace, with its well-preserved medieval streets and architectural treasures, exudes a tranquil ambiance that invites travelers to wander and discover its hidden corners. Lose yourself in the labyrinthine alleys, where each turn reveals a new architectural marvel. Admire the intricate details of the stone houses, the elegant archways, and the charming courtyards. The village's architecture reflects the influences of the Normans, Goths, and Byzantines, creating a unique blend of styles that adds to its allure.

A visit to Gerace is like stepping back in time. It allows you to immerse yourself in the authentic beauty and history of Calabria. As you explore this hidden gem, you'll be captivated by its rich heritage, picturesque surroundings, and the sense of tranquility that permeates the air. Gerace invites you to slow down, soak up its timeless atmosphere, and create memories that will last a lifetime.

In addition to its historical and architectural treasures, Gerace offers a wealth of experiences that further enhance the visit to this captivating village. As you meander through its streets, take the time to appreciate the unique blend of aromas that waft through the air. Gerace is known for its traditional artisan workshops, where skilled craftsmen continue age-old traditions. Stop by a pottery studio to witness the creation of beautiful ceramics or visit a local shoemaker to observe the meticulous craftsmanship that goes into making traditional leather goods.

For a deeper immersion into Gerace's cultural tapestry, consider timing your visit with one of the village's vibrant festivals. Throughout the year, Gerace comes alive with lively celebrations that showcase its rich traditions and local customs. The sounds of traditional music fill the air as locals and visitors gather to participate in processions, parades, and folklore performances. From religious festivals that pay homage to saints to culinary events that highlight regional specialties, these festive occasions offer a glimpse into the heart and soul of Gerace's community.

No visit to Gerace would be complete without indulging in the local gastronomy. Traditional Calabrian cuisine is known for its robust flavors and use of fresh, local ingredients. The village boasts charming trattorias and restaurants where you can savor authentic dishes that have been passed down through generations. Treat your taste buds to specialties like 'nduja (spicy spreadable salami), freshly made pasta, and hearty stews that showcase the region's agricultural bounty. Pair your meal with a glass of Calabrian wine, known for its robust character and distinctive flavors.

As the sun begins to set, find a tranquil spot to witness Gerace's transformation into a romantic wonderland. The golden hues of the fading sunlight cast a warm glow on the stone buildings, creating a magical ambiance. Take a moment to reflect on the timeless beauty of this hidden gem, surrounded by the echoes of history and the natural splendor of Calabria.

Whether you are a history enthusiast, a food lover, or a seeker of authentic experiences, Gerace invites you to embrace its enchantments. It offers a captivating blend of history, culture, and natural beauty that will leave an indelible mark on your journey through Calabria.

Pentedattilo

Nestled amidst the rugged landscape of Calabria, Pentedattilo emerges as a captivating ghost town that exudes an irresistible allure. Located in the southernmost region of Italy, Calabria is known for its dramatic landscapes, and Pentedattilo is no exception. Perched atop a rocky outcrop overlooking the picturesque valleys and the sparkling Ionian Sea, this abandoned village offers a mesmerizing blend of history, mystery, and natural beauty.

Pentedattilo's unique history adds an intriguing layer to its already captivating charm. Once a thriving medieval settlement, the town derived its name from the Greek words "pente" (meaning "five") and "daktylos" (meaning "fingers"). The name aptly describes the shape of the rock formation on which the village stands, resembling a hand with five outstretched fingers.

Walking through the narrow, winding streets of Pentedattilo, visitors can't help but feel the weight of the past. The village's history is filled with tales of bandits, nobility, and communal life. It was a place where locals worked, lived, and celebrated together, creating a vibrant community. However, in the late 19th century, due to economic decline and natural disasters, the residents gradually abandoned the village, leaving it frozen in time.

Today, Pentedattilo stands as a hauntingly beautiful ghost town, preserving the remnants of its storied past. As visitors explore the abandoned houses, churches, and other structures, they can catch glimpses of the lives once lived within these walls. The decaying facades and crumbling archways serve as poignant reminders of the village's former glory.

While the rich history of Pentedattilo is undeniably captivating, the natural beauty of its surroundings adds another layer of enchantment. The village's elevated position grants visitors awe-inspiring vistas that stretch far and wide. The rugged Calabrian landscape, with its undulating hills, olive groves, and vineyards, sprawls beneath the town. The azure waters of the Ionian Sea shimmer on the horizon, creating a striking contrast against the earthy tones of the land.

For those with a sense of adventure, hiking to the top of the rocky outcrop rewards them with even more breathtaking panoramas. Standing at the summit, visitors can take in the unique geological formations that have shaped Pentedattilo over time. The sheer cliffs, crevices, and weathered rocks present a natural spectacle, further enhancing the haunting beauty of the ghost town.

Whether you visit Pentedattilo for its intriguing history, its striking natural setting, or simply to immerse yourself in its eerie ambiance, the experience is bound to leave you in awe. This ghost town's ability to transport you to a bygone era, coupled with the captivating views that surround it, make Pentedattilo a must-visit destination for those seeking to uncover the secrets of Calabria's past.

The Ghost Town with a Unique History

Pentedattilo, which derives its name from the Greek words "penta" meaning "five" and "daktylos" meaning "fingers," is an enchanting village situated on a rocky outcrop that resembles a hand with five fingers. This unique geological formation is the defining characteristic of Pentedattilo and has contributed to its intriguing allure.

In its heyday, Pentedattilo was a bustling medieval village with a vibrant community. The strategic location of the town atop the rocky formation provided a natural defense against potential invaders, allowing the village to thrive and develop over the centuries. Its elevated position offered panoramic views of the surrounding landscape, including the sweeping valleys and the sparkling Ionian Sea.

However, as time passed and circumstances changed, the village's fortunes began to decline. In the late 19th century, a combination of factors, such as economic hardships, political instability, and emigration, led to the gradual abandonment of Pentedattilo. The once-flourishing village became a ghost town, frozen in time.

Today, wandering through the narrow, deserted streets of Pentedattilo is like stepping into a bygone era. As you explore the remnants of old houses, churches, and other structures, you can almost feel the echoes of the past. The weathered stone walls, worn staircases, and crumbling archways stand as silent witnesses to the village's rich history.

Pentedattilo's history is steeped in legends and tales that have been passed down through generations. These stories speak of bandits seeking refuge within the village's narrow alleys and caves, and noble families who once ruled over the region. Each crumbling building and abandoned courtyard holds secrets and whispers of the past, inviting visitors to delve into the mysteries of Pentedattilo.

The old houses, though dilapidated, retain their distinct architectural features, showcasing the craftsmanship of the past. From ornate doorways and intricate balconies to stone-carved details, these remnants provide glimpses into the daily lives of the villagers who once called Pentedattilo home. Exploring the town's structures allows visitors to connect with the stories and personal histories that are intertwined within its walls.

Pentedattilo's haunting beauty lies not only in its physical remnants but also in the sense of melancholic nostalgia that permeates the atmosphere. The combination of the village's scenic location, its rich history, and the eerily deserted streets creates a captivating experience for those who venture to explore this ghost town. Pentedattilo offers a unique opportunity to immerse oneself in the ambiance of a bygone era and to reflect on the passage of time.

As you wander through the narrow, deserted streets of Pentedattilo, the silence is palpable, and the tranquility of the surroundings envelops you. The absence of modern-day hustle and bustle allows for a profound connection with the past. Every step you take carries you further into the captivating history of the village.

The remnants of old houses offer glimpses into the lives of the villagers who once inhabited them. Imagine the laughter of families echoing through the now empty courtyards, the aroma of traditional Calabrian dishes wafting from the kitchens, and the sounds of artisans working diligently on their crafts. The architectural details, though weathered by time, still bear witness to the artistry and skill of the past.

The churches of Pentedattilo hold a particular allure. Step inside and be transported to a time when these sacred spaces were alive with worship and communal gatherings. Marvel at the faded frescoes adorning the walls, and let your imagination roam as you picture the fervent prayers and ceremonies that once filled these hallowed halls.

One cannot help but be captivated by the stories that surround Pentedattilo. Tales of noble families who held court within the village, tales of bandits seeking refuge among its labyrinthine streets, and tales of love and tragedy that unfolded against its dramatic backdrop. These legends are interwoven into the fabric of Pentedattilo, adding an air of mystery and intrigue to its ghostly charm.

Beyond its historical significance, Pentedattilo offers breathtaking panoramic views that further enhance its allure. From its elevated position, the village overlooks the picturesque Calabrian countryside, with its rolling hills, terraced vineyards, and shimmering blue sea in the distance. As you gaze out over the landscape, you can't help but appreciate the natural beauty that surrounds this hidden gem.

Visiting Pentedattilo is a journey of discovery—a chance to immerse yourself in the past and gain a deeper understanding of the region's cultural heritage. It is an opportunity to connect with a place where time seems to stand still, and where the whispers of history are still carried on the gentle breeze.

Pentedattilo invites you to be a part of its story, to walk its streets with reverence, and to appreciate the haunting beauty that emerges from its ruins. Prepare to be enchanted by this captivating ghost town, where the echoes of the past resonate with every step you take.

Breathtaking Views and Ruins

One of the highlights of visiting Pentedattilo is the sheer magnificence of the panoramic views it offers. As you ascend the rocky outcrop on which the town is perched, you'll be rewarded with a mesmerizing vista that stretches as far as the eye can see. The commanding position of Pentedattilo allows it to overlook the picturesque valleys, carpeted with lush vegetation and dotted with ancient olive groves. Beyond the rolling hills, the glistening waters of the Ionian Sea shimmer under the golden rays of the sun, creating a scene of unparalleled beauty.

The vistas from Pentedattilo are truly awe-inspiring and will leave you breathless. With each turn, you'll be treated to a new perspective, capturing the harmony between the rugged natural landscape and the remnants of human history. It's no wonder that this place has become a favorite among photographers who seek to capture the essence of Calabria's enchanting beauty.

As you wander through the ruins of Pentedattilo, you'll uncover the remnants of ancient buildings and architectural features that harken back to its illustrious past. These vestiges of civilization stand as silent witnesses to the town's former glory. Marvel at the sturdy stone walls that have weathered the test of time, testaments to the craftsmanship and dedication of the town's inhabitants. Walk through archways that once welcomed visitors and residents alike, evoking a sense of nostalgia and curiosity. Ascend staircases that lead to nowhere, their purpose now lost in the annals of history. Each step you take amidst the ruins immerses you further into the rich tapestry of Pentedattilo's past.

The atmospheric ambiance that pervades Pentedattilo adds an extra layer of mystique to the experience. The whispers of the wind seem to carry the echoes of long-forgotten voices, inviting you to immerse yourself in the town's history and tales. The juxtaposition of the decaying structures against the backdrop of the stunning natural beauty creates an unforgettable ambiance that transports you to another time.

For the adventurous souls, hiking to the top of the rock formation presents an opportunity for an even more breathtaking panorama. As you ascend, the landscape unfolds before you, revealing the intricate details of the unique geological formations that give Pentedattilo its distinct character. From this vantage point, you can appreciate the sheer grandeur of the surrounding mountains, the undulating valleys, and the vast expanse of the sea. It's a moment that inspires introspection and contemplation, allowing you to connect with the timeless allure of this captivating place.

As you continue your exploration of Pentedattilo, you'll find that the town's unique geological formations add an additional layer of intrigue to its already captivating character. The rock formation itself is a marvel to behold, with its jagged peaks and deep crevices telling a story of geological forces at play over countless millennia. The interplay of light and shadow on the rugged surfaces creates a dramatic spectacle, casting an ethereal glow over the surroundings.

As you hike to the top of the rock formation, you'll discover hidden nooks and crannies, revealing unexpected surprises along the way. Delicate wildflowers and resilient shrubs cling to the rocky cliffs, adding touches of vibrant color to the otherwise stark landscape. You might even encounter small wildlife, such as lizards or birds, gracefully navigating their way through this natural sanctuary.

Reaching the summit, you'll be rewarded with a panoramic view that stretches far beyond Pentedattilo itself. The vast expanse of the Ionian Sea extends as far as the eye can see, its sparkling waters beckoning you to embark on new adventures. The coastal towns and villages along the shoreline stand as silent witnesses to the ebb and flow of time, their charm blending seamlessly with the natural splendor of Calabria.

From this lofty vantage point, take a moment to soak in the tranquility and serenity that envelops Pentedattilo. The silence is broken only by the gentle breeze whispering through the valleys, creating a sense of peaceful solitude. It's a place that invites introspection and contemplation, allowing you to disconnect from the hectic pace of modern life and reconnect with the raw beauty of nature.

In the evening, as the sun begins its descent, the warm hues of twilight cast a magical spell over Pentedattilo. The landscape is transformed into a canvas painted with shades of gold, orange, and purple, evoking a sense of enchantment and wonder. It's a time when the past and present meld together, blurring the boundaries between reality and imagination.

As you bid farewell to Pentedattilo, you'll carry with you not only the memories of its panoramic views and ancient ruins but also a deeper appreciation for the harmonious coexistence of nature and human history. Pentedattilo is a place that leaves an indelible mark on the soul, reminding you of the enduring power of the past and the enduring beauty of the natural world.

Whether you're a history enthusiast, a photography lover, or simply seeking an offbeat destination, Pentedattilo is sure to captivate your imagination with its ghostly charm and mesmerizing views.

Stilo

Stilo, nestled in the heart of Calabria, is a truly picturesque town that exudes charm and beauty. As you venture into its narrow streets, lined with stone buildings and quaint houses, you'll be transported to another era. The town's well-preserved architecture and serene atmosphere create an ambiance that evokes a sense of stepping back in time.

One of the defining characteristics of Stilo is its rich historical and architectural heritage. The town proudly showcases its Byzantine past through various notable attractions. Each step you take reveals glimpses of the region's captivating history.

Among the town's treasures is the renowned Cattolica di Stilo, a magnificent Byzantine church that dates back to the 9th century. This architectural marvel stands as a testament to Stilo's importance during the Byzantine era. As you approach the church, you'll be greeted by its distinct octagonal shape, adorned with intricate details and decorative elements. The Cattolica di Stilo is a true masterpiece, reflecting the fusion of Byzantine and Arab influences that characterized the region's cultural landscape.

Within the church, you'll discover a world of artistic splendor. The interior is adorned with vibrant mosaics and captivating frescoes, depicting religious scenes and figures. The skill and craftsmanship displayed in these artworks are awe-inspiring, providing a glimpse into the rich artistic tradition of the time. As you wander through the halls of the Cattolica di Stilo, you'll feel a profound sense of reverence and admiration for the cultural heritage it represents.

Stilo's Old Town is another gem waiting to be explored. The labyrinthine streets wind their way through the town, revealing hidden corners and unexpected surprises. As you stroll along, you'll come across charming shops, inviting cafés, and traditional eateries serving authentic Calabrian cuisine. The Old Town is a living testament to Stilo's past, and the locals take great pride in preserving its unique character.

As you delve deeper into Stilo's history, you'll uncover stories of the people who once inhabited these streets. From merchants to artisans, each building and corner holds echoes of the past. Immerse yourself in the town's historical narrative as you walk through Stilo's Old Town, and let the sense of timelessness envelop you.

In Stilo, the blend of natural beauty, historical significance, and architectural splendor creates an experience that is both captivating and unforgettable. The town's ability to transport visitors to a bygone era makes it a must-visit destination for those seeking a glimpse into the region's Byzantine past. Stilo stands as a testament to Calabria's rich cultural heritage, inviting travelers to explore its hidden treasures and discover the magic of this remarkable town.

Cattolica di Stilo

The crown jewel of Stilo is undoubtedly the Cattolica di Stilo, an extraordinary Byzantine church that dates back to the 9th century. This architectural masterpiece is a testament to the rich history and cultural heritage of the region. As you approach the church, its striking presence and meticulous craftsmanship immediately capture your attention.

The Cattolica di Stilo stands as a prime example of the unique fusion of Byzantine and Arab influences that shaped the artistic traditions of Calabria. It is a true testament to the cultural diversity and exchange that characterized the region during that time.

One of the most remarkable features of the Cattolica di Stilo is its distinct octagonal shape. This design is a departure from the more common architectural forms seen in traditional Christian churches. The octagonal structure symbolizes the unity of the eight Beatitudes, adding a spiritual dimension to the architectural concept.

The church's exterior is adorned with intricate decorative details, showcasing the mastery of the craftsmen who brought it to life. Delicate carvings, geometric patterns, and intricate reliefs grace the facades, creating a mesmerizing visual experience. Each element tells a story and reflects the devotion and artistry of the people who built this remarkable place of worship.

Step inside the Cattolica di Stilo, and you'll be greeted by a serene and ethereal atmosphere. The interior is adorned with beautiful frescoes that depict religious scenes, saints, and biblical narratives. These vibrant and meticulously painted frescoes offer a glimpse into the artistic techniques and religious fervor of the Byzantine era.

As you explore the Cattolica di Stilo, take a moment to admire the delicate mosaics that embellish the walls and domed ceilings. These intricate mosaics are a testament to the exceptional craftsmanship of Byzantine artisans. The use of vibrant colors and meticulous attention to detail creates a truly captivating and awe-inspiring sight.

The Cattolica di Stilo stands as an enduring symbol of the region's artistic excellence and cultural diversity. It is a place where the past comes alive, allowing visitors to connect with the legacy of the Byzantine and Arab influences that shaped Calabria's history. A visit to this architectural gem is a journey through time, where you can appreciate the ingenuity, devotion, and creativity of those who came before us.

Every corner of the Cattolica di Stilo is steeped in history and symbolism. As you explore the church, you'll notice the intricate Byzantine-style iconostasis—a partition that separates the sanctuary from the nave. This beautifully adorned screen serves as a focal point for religious rituals and adds a layer of spiritual significance to the space.

The play of light within the Cattolica di Stilo is truly enchanting. The carefully positioned windows and openings allow the sunlight to filter through, casting a warm and ethereal glow on the frescoes and mosaics. It creates an ambiance of tranquility and invites contemplation.

The Cattolica di Stilo has witnessed centuries of events, including social, cultural, and religious transformations. It has stood resilient against the test of time, surviving earthquakes and changing architectural trends. It serves as a tangible link to the past, preserving the stories, traditions, and artistic achievements of the Byzantine era.

Beyond its architectural significance, the Cattolica di Stilo holds immense cultural and historical value for the people of Calabria. It serves as a place of pilgrimage, drawing both locals and visitors who seek solace, inspiration, and a connection to their roots. The church's spiritual aura transcends time, offering a sanctuary for reflection and introspection.

Visiting the Cattolica di Stilo is a transformative experience. It allows you to appreciate the beauty of art, the depth of faith, and the interconnectedness of cultures. It stands as a symbol of unity, reminding us that human creativity knows no bounds and that diverse influences can blend harmoniously to create something truly extraordinary.

In Stilo, the Cattolica di Stilo reigns supreme as an architectural gem that encapsulates the spirit and heritage of Calabria. Its allure and significance extend far beyond its physical structure. It represents the resilience, creativity, and cultural richness of the region—a treasure to be cherished and admired by generations to come.

Calabrian Byzantine Architecture

Stilo's Cattolica di Stilo stands as a magnificent testament to the Calabrian Byzantine architecture that flourished during the Byzantine era. This architectural style showcases a unique blend of influences from Byzantine and Arab cultures, resulting in a distinct and awe-inspiring aesthetic.

One of the defining features of Calabrian Byzantine architecture is the presence of domed roofs. These domes, often adorned with intricate patterns and designs, create a sense of grandeur and elegance. The domes are usually supported by sturdy columns or arches, adding to the structural integrity of the buildings.

Inside the Cattolica di Stilo, visitors are treated to a visual feast of mosaics and ornate frescoes that grace the interior walls. Mosaics are created by carefully arranging small colored tiles or glass pieces to form intricate patterns and images. These mosaics often depict religious scenes, saints, and biblical stories, showcasing the rich spiritual heritage of the region.

The ornate frescoes further enhance the beauty of the interior. Frescoes are paintings executed on freshly laid plaster, allowing the colors to seep into the plaster and become an integral part of the wall itself. The frescoes in Stilo's Cattolica di Stilo exhibit a high level of craftsmanship and detail, depicting scenes from the life of Christ, the Virgin Mary, and other religious figures.

Calabrian Byzantine architecture left a profound legacy in the region, with numerous religious structures that have stood the test of time. These architectural gems dot the Calabrian landscape, inviting visitors to marvel at their beauty and experience a connection with the past. They serve as a reminder of the rich cultural heritage of Calabria and its significant role in the Byzantine Empire.

Visiting Stilo's Cattolica di Stilo allows travelers to immerse themselves in the splendor of Calabrian Byzantine architecture. It offers a glimpse into a bygone era, where art, faith, and architectural ingenuity converged to create masterpieces that continue to inspire awe and admiration.

Stilo Old Town

Stilo's Old Town beckons visitors with its enchanting atmosphere and well-preserved architectural wonders. As you step into this labyrinth of winding alleys and stone houses, you'll find yourself transported to a bygone era. The narrow cobblestone streets wind their way through the heart of the town, creating a sense of mystery and intrigue.

Wandering through the Old Town, you'll come across charming shops that line the streets. These quaint establishments offer a treasure trove of local products, handicrafts, and souvenirs. Delight in the discovery of unique keepsakes, intricately crafted ceramics, traditional textiles, and artisanal jewelry. The local shopkeepers are friendly and eager to share stories about their wares, providing insight into the town's cultural heritage.

As you continue your exploration, tantalizing aromas waft from traditional eateries that dot the streets. These inviting establishments serve up authentic Calabrian cuisine, showcasing the region's culinary traditions. Take a break from your stroll and savor the flavors of homemade pasta dishes, freshly caught seafood, and mouthwatering local specialties.

Conclusion

Embracing the Enchantments of Calabria

In this final chapter, we invite you to embark on a reflective journey, immersing yourself in the enchantments of Calabria and cherishing the unforgettable experiences that have shaped your travel adventure. Calabria, with its unspoiled landscapes, hidden gems, and deep-rooted cultural heritage, has undoubtedly left an indelible mark on your heart and travel memories.

Throughout your exploration of Calabria, you have been captivated by the region's natural beauty and diverse offerings. The breathtaking coastlines have bewitched you with their turquoise waters, pristine beaches, and dramatic cliffs that seem to plunge into the Mediterranean Sea. Whether you lounged under the warm sun, took refreshing dips in the crystal-clear waters, or embarked on thrilling water sports, the coastlines of Calabria have offered moments of tranquility and exhilaration.

Beyond the coastal allure, Calabria's historic towns have invited you to step back in time and witness the rich tapestry of Italy's hidden gem. Strolling through ancient streets and squares, you have discovered architectural wonders that stand as testaments to centuries of history. The well-preserved castles, churches, and palaces have shared tales of conquerors, artists, and visionaries who have shaped the region's identity.

From the hilltop town of Tropea, with its charming cathedral and panoramic views, to the vibrant city of Reggio Calabria, home to the renowned Museo Nazionale della Magna Grecia, you have marveled at the convergence of cultures and the echoes of the past. Each town has unfolded a unique chapter of Calabria's story, inviting you to delve deeper into its secrets.

But it is not just the grandeur of the landscapes and the richness of history that have enchanted you; it is the essence of Calabria itself. The warmth and friendliness of the local people, their unwavering pride in their heritage, and their dedication to preserving age-old traditions have added a layer of authenticity to your journey. Conversations shared over a cup of strong espresso, joining in local festivals and celebrations, and savoring the region's delectable cuisine have allowed you to connect with the heart and soul of Calabria.

As you reflect on your time in Calabria, you realize that this journey has been more than just a vacation. It has been an immersive experience that has broadened your understanding of a region often overshadowed by its more renowned counterparts. Calabria has revealed itself as a treasure trove of hidden gems, awaiting the discerning traveler willing to venture off the beaten path.

The allure of Italy's hidden gem, Calabria, lies not only in its breathtaking coastlines and historic towns but also in the indescribable feeling of connection and appreciation that it evokes. The memories you have made, the stories you have collected, and the moments of wonder you have experienced will forever be cherished. Calabria has gifted you with a profound sense of discovery and a newfound appreciation for the lesser-known wonders that lie off the tourist trail.

As you turn the final page of this travel guide, may the enchantments of Calabria continue to inspire your wanderlust and ignite a desire to seek out the hidden gems that await you in your future travels.

Final Tips and Recommendations

As you conclude your Calabria adventure, we would like to offer some practical tips and recommendations to make the most of your time in this captivating region:

Capture the Moments: Remember to take plenty of photographs to capture the beauty and essence of Calabria. The region is known for its stunning landscapes, picturesque coastlines, and charming towns. From the rugged mountains of Sila National Park to the turquoise waters of the Ionian Sea, every corner of Calabria offers a unique backdrop for capturing breathtaking images. Don't forget to document the vibrant local culture, from colorful festivals and traditional dances to lively street markets and historic landmarks. These photographs will serve as cherished mementos, allowing you to relive the sights and emotions of your Calabria journey for years to come.

Immerse Yourself in the Culture: One of the most rewarding aspects of traveling to Calabria is the opportunity to engage with the locals and immerse yourself in the region's rich culture. Take the time to learn a few basic Italian phrases and embrace the warm hospitality of Calabria. Strike up conversations with the locals, whether it's at a family-owned trattoria or a bustling piazza. They will gladly share their stories, traditions, and insights into the region's way of life. By connecting with the people of Calabria, you will gain a deeper understanding of their customs, values, and the authentic spirit that defines the region.

Try Local Cuisine: Calabria is a paradise for food lovers, and no visit to the region would be complete without indulging in its tantalizing cuisine. Calabrian gastronomy is renowned for its bold flavors and emphasis on locally sourced ingredients. Take the opportunity to savor traditional dishes such as pasta alla norma, which features eggplant and ricotta salata, or enjoy a plate of fresh seafood along the coast. Be sure to sample 'nduja, a spicy spreadable salami that is a specialty of the region. Explore the vibrant food markets where you can find an array of regional delicacies, including olives, cheeses, cured meats, and homemade pastries. By immersing yourself in the flavors of Calabria, you will not only satisfy your taste buds but also gain a deeper appreciation for the region's culinary heritage.

Embrace Nature: Calabria is blessed with an abundance of natural wonders, making it an ideal destination for nature enthusiasts. Take advantage of the region's diverse landscapes by embarking on outdoor adventures. Explore the vast national parks, such as Sila National Park and Aspromonte National Park, where you can hike through lush forests, spot rare wildlife, and breathe in the fresh mountain air. Calabria's coastline offers pristine beaches and crystal-clear waters, perfect for swimming, sunbathing, and water sports. Whether you choose to go trekking, mountain biking, or simply take a leisurely stroll along the shore, immersing yourself in Calabria's stunning landscapes will awaken your senses and rejuvenate your spirit.

Respect the Environment: Calabria's natural beauty is a precious resource that should be treasured and preserved for future generations. When exploring the region's outdoor spaces, it is essential to be mindful of the environment. Follow designated trails and respect any guidelines or restrictions in place to protect fragile ecosystems. Dispose of waste properly by using designated trash bins or taking it with you to be disposed of later. Consider adopting sustainable travel practices, such as using reusable water bottles and reducing single-use plastic. By being a responsible traveler, you contribute to the preservation of Calabria's natural environment, ensuring that future visitors can also enjoy its pristine landscapes.

Fond Farewell to Calabria

As you bid farewell to Calabria, allow yourself a moment to pause and reflect on the incredible experiences and memories that have become an integral part of your journey. Whether you embarked on solo adventures or shared the wonders of Calabria with loved ones, each encounter has shaped your perception of this captivating region.

Cherish the friendships you formed along the way, as the warmth and hospitality of the Calabrian people have undoubtedly left an imprint on your heart. From the locals who shared their stories and traditions to fellow travelers with whom you exchanged tales of exploration, these connections have enriched your travel experience and expanded your horizons.

As you reminisce, the landscapes of Calabria will come alive in your mind's eye. The majestic cliffs plunging into the azure Mediterranean Sea, the golden beaches stretching as far as the eye can see, and the rugged mountains cloaked in lush greenery—all of these natural wonders have etched themselves into your memories. Allow the tranquility of the rolling countryside and the vibrant hues of the sunset to linger, knowing that Calabria's beauty will forever be a source of inspiration.

Beyond the physical landscapes, reflect on the cultural heritage you embraced during your time in Calabria. The echoes of ancient civilizations, from the Greeks to the Romans, are woven into the fabric of the region. The magnificent architecture, the archeological sites, and the museums filled with treasures from the past have offered you a glimpse into Calabria's rich history. By immersing yourself in the local traditions, tasting the authentic flavors of Calabrian cuisine, and participating in cultural festivities, you have deepened your connection to this land and its people.

As you prepare to leave Calabria, carry the spirit of this enchanting region with you. Let the lessons learned and the transformative experiences serve as a compass for your future travels. The open-mindedness, curiosity, and sense of adventure that Calabria has instilled in you will guide you on new paths and inspire your wanderlust to explore other destinations.

Although you may be departing Calabria's shores, know that the enchantments of this hidden gem will continue to resonate within you. The memories you have crafted will endure, providing a wellspring of inspiration and fond recollections. Remember to share your stories with others, spreading the magic of Calabria and igniting the curiosity of fellow travelers.

Safe travels on your onward journey, and may the enchantments of Calabria forever whisper in your ear, urging you to return one day. There will always be more to explore, more hidden treasures to uncover, and more moments of awe awaiting your arrival in the heart of Italy.

Printed in Great Britain
by Amazon

25533816R00089